your
child
your
way

Other titles by Dr Tanya Byron

The House of Tiny Tearaways
Little Angels

Look out for Dr Tanya Byron's podcast, available
at www.penguin.co.uk/yourchildyourway

If you would like to receive more information on Healthy
Penguin titles, authors, special offers, events and giveaways,
please email HealthyPenguin@uk.penguingroup.com

DR TANYA BYRON

your child your

Create a positive parenting pattern for life

PENGUIN
MICHAEL
JOSEPH

MICHAEL JOSEPH

Published by the Penguin Group
Penguin Books Ltd, 80 Strand, London WC2R ORL, England
Penguin Group (USA) Inc., 375 Hudson Street, New York, New York 10014, USA
Penguin Group (Canada), 90 Eglinton Avenue East, Suite 700, Toronto, Ontario, Canada M4P 2Y3
(a division of Pearson Penguin Canada Inc.)
Penguin Ireland, 25 St Stephen's Green, Dublin 2, Ireland (a division of Penguin Books Ltd)
Penguin Group (Australia), 250 Camberwell Road,
Camberwell, Victoria 3124, Australia (a division of Pearson Australia Group Pty Ltd)
Penguin Books India Pvt Ltd, 11 Community Centre,
Panchsheel Park, New Delhi – 110 017, India
Penguin Group (NZ), 67 Apollo Drive, Rosedale, North Shore 0632, New Zealand
(a division of Pearson New Zealand Ltd)
Penguin Books (South Africa) (Pty) Ltd, 24 Sturdee Avenue,
Rosebank, Johannesburg 2196, South Africa

Penguin Books Ltd, Registered Offices: 80 Strand, London WC2R ORL, England

www.penguin.com

Published in 2007

1

Text copyright © Dr Tanya Byron, 2007
Illustrations copyright © Kipper Williams, 2007

Designed and typeset by Smith & Gilmour, London

Printed in Great Britain by Clays Ltd, St Ives plc

A CIP catalogue record for this book is available from the British Library

ISBN: 978–0–718–15150–8

For Lily and Jack, who are teaching
me everything I know.

And for Bruce, my wonderful co-pilot
on this extraordinary journey.

CONTENTS

FOREWORD

I am both a parent and a consultant in clinical psychology
specializing in work with children, young people and their
families. For many years I have worked with a variety of families
who, for one reason or another, have become unhappy living
together and have struggled to find a way through the difficulties,
the arguments and the sadness. Using a variety of techniques –
behaviour therapy, cognitive therapy, cognitive behaviour therapy
and family therapy approaches – I, and many valued colleagues,
have worked towards finding the best combination of approaches
and techniques to meet the needs of each family. No two families
are the same and there is no 'one size fits all' approach that can
magically solve the problems that families face.

However, with an upsurge in interest in the theories of
parenting, we are living in a time of real confusion. A variety
of parenting theories, books, articles and television programmes
aim to enable parents to find the 'right way' to manage their
child's behaviour but seem in fact to muddle and disempower.
Parents are overwhelmed by advice and tips from an industry
growing out of the most basic and instinctive aspect of life –
child rearing.

I have become part of this industry in writing books and
making television programmes about children and families with
behaviour problems. On television, I have worked with some
incredible families who have bravely worked through some of
their issues in public and who have not only resolved their own
difficulties but also enabled others to learn how to as well. My
work on television has always come from an evidence-based
perspective as a professionally trained clinician who is qualified
to work with children and families. However, as the success of
the media parenting industry grows, I find that the mothers and
fathers whom I meet each week in my clinics seem more and
more confused. It seems that despite the overwhelming amount

of information that is available many parents seem saturated to the point where they feel unable to make use of what they watch or read. Many ask me whether they should favour one technique over another or tell me that they have tried every method available but 'nothing works'. So it seems there is a generation of parents who have an intellectual understanding of the 'correct' parenting techniques and approaches but have no real emotional understanding of how to make them work for their child.

This seems to be a big issue because it's one thing to be struggling with a problem because you genuinely have no real idea what to do, but it all becomes significantly worse if you are still struggling despite knowing everything that there is to do. And so whereas in my early years as a practitioner I would work with families who were unclear on how to manage certain behaviours, now I am working with parents who know exactly what to do but still can't manage it.

Why is this? Well, my belief is that the 'parenting industry' is marketing a simplified and unrealistic view of parenting, which is based on the notion that to be a parent is a series of problems to be solved and techniques to be mastered. But, if that really were the case, why do so many parents feel inadequate? Can being a parent really be only a combination of a few 'quick and easy' tips and techniques? Is it a role that involves a series of tasks in order to 'get it right'? Can parenting be that simple? Well, from my own experience I would answer absolutely not – and I say this as a parent not a practitioner. You see, with all my years of training and experience, you would think that I am breezing through the upbringing of my own two children, who are themselves impeccably behaved and developmentally way above average. With a mother like me who knows all the theory – every trick in the book (she's already written two) – surely my children are models of the best-parented children.

Well, actually, no – they are not.

My daughter had a sleep problem. I knew what to do: I'd written the paper; I was trained to deal with it. But, standing over her cot at four o'clock in the morning looking at this little person whom I loved more than anything else, whom I would lay my own life down for, there was no way I could do anything (despite my desperate and exhausted husband begging me to). She was mine and, despite knowing all the techniques there were, my emotions, my overwhelming love and protectiveness for her stopped logic, stopped reason and compelled me to pick her up and hold her close despite knowing it was the 'wrong' thing to do.

So although I am a practitioner, knowing all the theory – all the theo*ries* – of child development, I also struggle with my children's behaviour. And I have found that if I automatically try to go to the prescriptive elements of what I know, even I, as the expert in innumberable case studies and in every what if, yes and but (because I've seen it all in my sixteen years of working in this field), still don't get it right with my own kids. So as well as knowing the techniques there has to be something else – something that this age of 'getting it right' has destroyed.

Actually, I don't want my children to be 'perfect' compliant little people with no spark of personality, no ability to say 'NO!' and mean it, no sense of rage when they perceive injustice – I want them to have all those qualities in order for them to survive in this tough and exacting world. However, to get them to that point my husband and I will have to weather the development of the stubborn streak and deal with the early rages, the sulks, the defiance, the non-compliance. We will have to because that is our role – to guide our children through these early emotional and behavioural experiences and, with compassion, help them learn how to have those feelings and behave in a way that also allows them to live and communicate as social beings.

And that is what this book is about – knowing the techniques but most importantly knowing your individual child and having an instinctive connection to what works for them and for you in this, the most incredible relationship you will ever have. It's about understanding their development as a series of challenges for your child and for you as their parent, and for these challenges to be celebrated rather than seen as negative moments, as hard work. It is about having the courage to let your child be when it feels right without worrying about what others say.

This book is about combining thinking and emotion – knowing the techniques and then instinctively finding the way to make them work positively for you and your child. Fundamentally, it is about getting back to enjoying parenting as the most incredible few years of your life – for that's what they are and that's how they should feel: a pleasure and a privilege.

Note about language: The words 'parent' or 'parents' will be used throughout this book to represent the significant individual(s) and carer(s) in your child's life.

INTRODUCTION

Your child. Your way?

Why do we need a book to tell us how to do what should be the most instinctive part of our lives? There is so much parenting information and advice out there that is confusing and disempowering. The aim of this book is to help you really think about the kind of parent you are and the kind of parent you want to be, but mostly to understand your child, because once you *understand* their behaviour's meaning, you'll be able to manage it.

This book is not about superficial problem solving, so it's not a prescriptive approach to parenting, although I will offer practical guidance wherever possible. It's about starting off a process that will enable you to manage the first stage of your child's development where their behaviour will be challenging, which is as a toddler, and then find a way of relating to them and their behaviour to set up a positive pattern for the whole of your relationship as a parent rather than just in the short term. You can use this book to help solve some difficulties you are currently experiencing or just to help you think about how you want to parent your child – this book is aimed at anyone with a child and can help prevent behaviour problems as well as solve them but most importantly allow you to define the parent you want to be and to be the expert on your child.

So it's about understanding your child, and more importantly understanding the way you respond to your child based on your own history and personality. And to avoid getting into a notion that there is always a quick fix, understanding that sometimes there are no answers and that's OK. And at times when there are answers it's important to implement the strategies in a way that, yes, in the short term will solve the problems, but also in the longer term will form the kind of relationship you have with your child.

However, I realize that you might be opening this book exhausted and looking for solutions. To a lesser or greater degree you might find yourself caught in a negative cycle with your child where you feel that you are not relating as you want to, that your child is out of control or that you've lost your confidence and just don't feel like a good parent. That's why the first two parts of this book will enable you to break out of that negative cycle and get solving practical problems. So, for example, if your child has a sleep problem – maybe they're in your bed – I will show you what steps you can take to change that pattern and get your child sleeping happily in their own bed. Or, how to reduce the tantrums, or have them eating more confidently, or using the potty without a fuss.

But it's essential to go further than solve the initial problem. As a psychologist, I know that unless you really understand how that problem started in the first place and address that your child will soon be back in your bed/throwing huge tantrums/refusing to eat/not using the potty – or whatever your specific difficulty is. There are three key steps in this process: 'What is the problem?', 'What do you do?' and 'Why was it a problem in the first place?'. By addressing the third stage you can maintain the change.

Each and every child is unique, so therefore it is slightly ludicrous to expect a singular approach to managing children to be the way to go. You need to bring a great deal to this process yourself, take the different blocks and put them together in a way that works for you and your family.

The greatest chefs know that every time they cook the same dish it tastes slightly different, because the ingredients change in flavour just slightly each time, but they understand their raw materials so well that they will add a pinch more of this or a pinch less of that to make the dish work. You need to be just as flexible and sensitive and open when approaching the most important relationship of your life, which is your relationship with your child and your child's relationship with you.

My hope is that by the end of this book you will have a clearer understanding of child behaviour and positive, practical psychological and behavioural management techniques for the times when you need to help your child learn. More importantly, however, I hope that your experience of reading this book gives you the confidence to take ownership of being your child's parent so that you can implement these strategies in a way that works for you and your child within the context of a loving and nurturing relationship. This relationship between your child and you, their parent, is totally unique and therefore you are the key person who has the real instincts about your child when it comes to their parenting.

Because much of the parenting information available is confusing and leaves you feeling that you are actually the least able person to parent your child I've written this book to be different – this book is about parenting your child, your way.

What is it to be a parent?
'Good or not, we're the only ones they've got.'

During the writing of this book I did a number of focus groups with parents because I felt that I wanted to really understand the current preoccupations that the parents of young children struggle with. In each group, what first struck me was the sense that the members were sitting and waiting for me – the expert – to tell them what they were 'doing wrong' and how they could 'get it right'. These experiences underlined to me even more that what we all need as parents is the permission to take a step back and think less about the superficial solutions to parenting (such as which technique we should use for which behaviour) and more about the core aspects of being a parent that comes with our attitudes and beliefs about ourselves, our children and our families. It was interesting to find how the groups relaxed once we all agreed that there is no 'right way', there is no 'one size fits all' approach to parenting and that in the same way we don't

approach other significant relationships with a prescriptive sense
of when and how we communicate, nor should we do so with our
parenting. Being an effective parent is underpinned by a set of
positive and confident beliefs – hard to achieve when we are
feeling so dazed and confused:

*'As soon as your baby is born, you've got the midwife
telling you how to do this, how to do that; you go to courses
and classes beforehand as if there's just one right way to do
it. And then you even have your parents or your brother all
telling you how to do something, but it's never that simple.
I mean techniques that they think should work, might work
with one but not the other.'*

*'It's not natural to be a parent any more. It's like being
a robot, something you do automatically. Do this method,
follow that technique – you don't have to think about it
yourself any more.'*

*'I think there's too much choice when it comes to advice but
then if someone said to me there was one choice, I wouldn't
believe them, because I don't think that one particular
discipline works all the time or works on every child.'*

*'We can get so obsessed with getting it right that we can
actually set ourselves up to get it wrong.'*

*'You try one thing after another, and it doesn't work, then
you think, Oh no, what am I going to do now? I've tried
everything; there's nothing I can do. It makes you feel like
you're a bad parent.'*

*'I think there's a certain amount of pressure on parents to
be perfect, have the perfect child. It's not ever going to be like
that. You've just got to try your best and see what works for*

you, but there is so much pressure from other parents or family or the media.'

'It's like you're meant to have a textbook baby. No wonder we're all so neurotic – from the moment when you first fall pregnant, you're told you're not to smoke, not to do this, not to eat that. And then breastfeeding is best. You can feel guilty and inadequate almost from day one.'

'I've got a daughter of eleven and a son of eight, and my personal feeling is that my children are completely different characters: what works for my daughter doesn't always work for my son, and vice versa, and if you try to take some kind of formula, and say this is the way to do it, it's going to fail because children are children and they're individuals.'

That last quote is me. At times we all feel overwhelmed, confused and paranoid about our abilities as parents. We all resent the conflicting information thrown at us, and how it seems to confuse rather than inform. It leaves us feeling less able and less in control. Yet we continue to watch the programmes and buy the books because what we also experience is a profound sense that there must be a 'right' way, a 'magic' answer, if only we could find it.

It's nonsense. We are all trapped in the marketing executives' dream and are lining the pockets of those who have found a way of turning this most natural process into something that we can buy off the shelf. In the same way that we have become trapped into the notion that by buying gym membership and a number of slimming magazines we can lose weight and feel better about ourselves, we are beginning to believe that being a great parent comes from a book or television programme. My career working as a clinician with children and their families has taught me that the issues involved are complex and unique to each individual. In this age of the quick fix, I am increasingly concerned that the 'parenting approaches' offered via television, books and articles are becoming so slick and glossy that they are missing the fundamental point – the issue at the heart of each and any family difficulty – that it's all about relationships and about the thoughts and feelings we have for each other.

Feeling good about oneself as a parent and about one's child, in the same way as feeling good and healthy about one's diet and body, comes with an examination of ourselves and who we are (our thoughts and feelings about ourselves) and not just a number of superficial behaviour changes. If we overeat, for example, unless we examine the role that food plays in our life (comfort, for example) and address the emotions that are behind our eating behaviour, we will only manage to stop overeating in the short term until will power runs out and our feelings of emptiness and failure kick back in. Unless we look at why we cannot parent our child in a way that feels positive and consistent even when they are being at their most challenging (because they are children and that is what children do), any 'parenting behaviour programmes' will only enable us to effect change in the short term until things slide back to where they were and – as with the moment we binge on a packet of biscuits and 'break the diet' – we begin to feel like a failure again.

In life, information can only empower if the person reading it is in the correct frame of mind to use it in a way that works for them. But, if we are trapped in a mindset that causes us to seek out the information because we feel insecure and negative about ourselves and our abilities, that information will do nothing for us as we will use it in an anxious, rigid and ineffective manner. As we all know from different experiences throughout our lives, the times that we have approached an issue to be tackled or mastered in a positive frame of mind, underpinned by a belief that we will succeed despite any challenges along the way, we not only accomplish those goals but also do so with pleasure even if at times the going got tricky.

Parenting cannot be learned in a step-by-step recipe-book

approach that guarantees the best-slept, best-fed, best-behaved child. It is a process that requires courage and flexibility, the ability to not always understand and to make mistakes, an attitude underpinned by fun and enthusiasm. It is a process that is unpredictable, exciting and frightening – the greatest experience of our lives.

I realize that I am not offering you a quick fix – but, if you are up for thinking beyond the quick-fix solutions to ensure longer-term success and happiness for all – for solving the immediate challenge with your young child but also for laying down the foundations for a healthy and strongly bonded relationship with your child for the many further challenges that come with their development – then this is your book. You *will* find approaches and techniques that, applied with positive attitudes and beliefs, will make a real difference to your child, yourself and your family. However, these techniques will only work in the long term if they are used as part of a process that requires a great deal of emotional thinking on your part. This book will ask you the questions to enable you to do the emotional thinking that will give you the fundamental confidence to be a parent – a confidence that will remain even when your child is challenging you at other times in their (and your) development because of a central belief that you have in the relationship and because of the respect that exists between you.

So, what kind of parent are you?

Although many of you will have thought, Not a very good one, to the question above, I urge you to think further. This book hasn't been written for 'bad' parents and 'bad' children. It's been written for confused and anxious parents and their children who are possibly feeling quite similar things. You have bought this book because you see me as the 'expert' who – if you read hard enough and really concentrate (despite the fact that you're exhausted and

would rather be watching telly with a glass of something chilled)
will give you the magic answer you've been looking for. You're
hoping for flow charts and bullet points, diagrams and neatly
boxed-off sections with case studies; you want easy-to-follow,
step-by-step, totally successful idiot-proof management plans.
But let me ask you this: haven't you already got lots of those
books on your shelves and aren't you still feeling confused, some
of you possibly feeling worse – out of control and unable to cope?
I'd say that you are but that your anxiety drives you on to read
further, make more notes, compile more lists, stick up more
charts and try, if it kills you, to find the magic answer. Well,
the truth is that if those approaches worked you wouldn't have
wanted to buy this book, so maybe there has to be another way.

I suspect you may find that concept quite challenging and
it may make some of you feel rather panic stricken but actually
the good news is that you don't need a book to tell you what to
do because inside yourself you actually have a very good idea.
No, you need a book to enable you to relax enough to allow
you to be that parent – the parent who instinctively knows what
works and what doesn't for their child; the parent who allows
themselves and their child to sometimes not know; the parent
who believes that they are the expert when it comes to parenting
their child above anybody else.

So what kind of parent are you? You are the best parent
your child could have. You are the parent who raises your child,
your way.

My hope is that this book will help to get you there.

Motivation: getting ourselves into the right mental space

The first stage of our journey together is very simply to get out of any negative mindset you may have about you or your child by finding ways to think and feel positively about your relationship, despite the current behaviour that might be going on. Because you are probably feeling somewhat confused and in a muddle about the way things are, you are probably exhausted and can't see the wood for the trees, I am going to guide you through a process that will enable you to feel less anxious and pessimistic and more positively set up for making real and lasting changes.

Once you have decided there is a problem, it is vital to monitor it and understand how it plays out before you try to solve it – that way you are going to feel more in control. However, before that, the first important step is to get in the right frame of mind to understand and solve the difficulties that you and your child are experiencing because, if you come at this from a belief that 'my child is a problem', then your child will remain a problem. If you label your child as 'a monster, out of control, a nightmare, difficult to handle, rules the roost, in charge of us, in charge of me', then while you continue to hold those beliefs your child will continue to be that individual. It's called the *self-fulfilling prophecy*: your beliefs about an individual or situation are transmitted through your behaviour towards them, which then sets them up to behave in the way you expect.

The first thing to say is, it is entirely normal to feel confused and anxious because parenting is the most challenging aspect of life – but you have to decide whether you see it as a positive series of challenges to be faced with enthusiasm and joy or as a difficult and arduous series of time-consuming and frustrating tasks. Therefore, my second point is that you have to really think a lot about the way you view both your child as an individual and yourself as a parent right now because those attitudes and beliefs will be driving what is currently going on: the good parts and the problems.

But if we actually look at this from the point of view of 'your child is bringing a challenge into your life', which every child does to every parent, and you are going to approach this with the same positive motivation that you would other challenges in your life that aren't so emotionally laden, then you will succeed. Because you are coming at it in the right way. I can give you every technique in the world, but, unless you're in the right frame of mind to use them, nothing will work.

To help you understand this better, here is an example of how an underlying belief will impact significantly on our thoughts, feelings and behaviour and thus impact directly on our child's behaviour. In this example, you the parent have a very anxious and negative view of your child and their behaviour:

You've been invited over to a friend's house for a children's birthday party. Because of how your child has behaved at such gatherings before, you are stressed and anxious before you even walk through the door. As you get to the party you find it impossible to relax and also feel that others are looking at you and your child and expecting there to be a problem – you feel judged and insecure. All the while you are on red alert – literally waiting to see what your child is going to do and waiting to pounce on them at the first sign of trouble. So you hop around them and hover nervously and every time they look at something or pick something up you leap on them verbally or physically because you are so afraid that they're going to break something. However, like everyone else in the room, your child will also pick up on all that stress and anxiety and this of course will increase their agitation and their stress. Then naturally your stress will rocket through the roof and your child will continue to pick up on and feed into how you, and in turn they, are feeling. Clearly it won't be long before their behaviour falls apart as, it is highly likely, will yours. In this scenario, therefore, your negative beliefs and resulting behaviours will have given your child a huge amount of negative attention and thus you are responsible if they behave in a negative way.

On the occasions that your child is behaving well, what do you do? Many parents tell me they don't want to go anywhere near their child during these times because they are frightened that if they say or do anything they will set them off. So they leave the child alone at these times and just let them be, and will often use the time, quite understandably, to run around and do some work in the house, or make phone calls or pay a bill or give attention to other siblings who usually get left out because this child takes up so much time and attention.

So this 'monster' of yours gets no attention when they are behaving wonderfully and absolutely tons of attention when they are being that 'monster'.

How we affect our children's behaviour

How is this relevant? Well, the first rule of understanding your child's behaviour is via a basic psychological model. The response you give to an action will determine whether that action is strengthened and continues or is extinguished over time. Your actions and reactions as a parent are fundamentally linked to how your child learns to behave in all areas of their developing lives. If, for example, your child is refusing to eat and you respond hugely to that either by shouting back at them or opening twenty-five packets of food to try to tempt them with something else, you are purely reinforcing (highlighting, emphasizing and strengthening) the non-eating, faddy behaviour, and so making it more likely to continue.

Your response to your child's behaviour is called a reinforcer, i.e., what you're doing is that by giving the behaviour you don't want a huge amount of attention you're actually making it more likely to reoccur because your child is being shown that this is the most effective way to get your attention. Couple that with not really attending to the lovely behaviour – because you don't want to disrupt it or stop it happening or you need to get on with other tasks – and your child will learn to produce the behaviours that bring the most attention, whatever form that attention takes. If the only way they're going to get it is by screaming and shouting, that's just what they'll do.

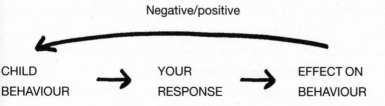

Negative/positive

CHILD BEHAVIOUR → YOUR RESPONSE → EFFECT ON BEHAVIOUR

Once you understand this concept, you're more than halfway there. A toddler can get used to this set up very easily. And when you find yourself in this cycle it's very hard to see the situation for what it is and find a way out. So, although you might be desperate for me to just give you the answers to your questions – How do I get my child to sleep through the night? How do I get them to behave in a more positive way? How can I stop my children beating each other up? – I say to you that you can't put any 'parenting technique' into practice successfully until you've changed your attitude (a) to your child and (b) to yourself as a parent. And sometimes that's all it takes.

This is why, before trying to change the behaviour, you must really have an intricate understanding of how that behaviour plays out between you and your child. To help you with this before I attempt to 'treat' a problem (and I include the parent as very much part of 'the problem'), I encourage a period of self-monitoring. If you try to move immediately to 'solving' the problem by skipping to the techniques section, you will very likely fail because your attempts will be superficial and not built on any real insight about the issues themselves. Please heed my words!

Right now, if your child is seen as being the most powerful person in the family, then your child will retain the power, whatever techniques you try. You need to start to feel positive in yourself as a parent, and confident and hopeful that you can effect a change, and that might be a big shift. When it comes from your heart, when it's real and grounded rather than superficial, your child will follow. This comes from a deep belief where you know 'I can be in charge again; I can be in control; I can teach, help, guide my child to sleep through the night...'

How can you shift into this positive frame of mind?

In my clinical practice this is a common scenario: I'll be doing a consultation with parents and little Timmy or little Jessica is drawing and playing nicely in the corner of my consultation room and I'll point out to the parents that their child, the devil they are describing to me as they wring their hands in despair, has been there for five minutes being delightful and the parents have made no comment or interaction with them – they've said nothing. And so often these parents will say to me, 'Well, you just wait – s/he will show their true colours soon,' and I have to ask myself – well who's the adult here? Who is the person who has the powers of reasoning and logical thought?

Often I will then ask the parents to tell me three things about their child, and they'll give me two negatives, followed by a quick 'oh, but they've got a really lovely personality' kind of thing. This reflects to me very simply how the parents have become stuck in a predominantly negative mindset about their child and as we have thought about earlier – if you think negatively about your child, your child will behave negatively.

Try this exercise:

STEP 1

Make two lists about your child – one that lists all their lovely attributes and another that lists the less desirable qualities that you and others find difficult. If you are parenting with a partner do this separately and then compare and contrast. In my experience most parents who come to me (if they are being really honest with me and themselves) will have a much longer negative-quality list. Reflect on this for a moment – why is this the case? Is your child really a mostly unpleasant, difficult person? Is this who they really are? Or does this reflect something (a) about how those around them have become more attuned to their problematic qualities and behaviours and/or (b) that their behaviour reflects their age and stage of development.

Repeat this exercise with a list of your parenting qualities: those you perceive as positive and negative – and if you have a partner try this exercise on each other.

STEP 2

Now sit down with a piece of paper and write down five great things about your child and five great things about you as a parent. And why you are lucky to have your child and why your child is lucky to have you as a parent. This is called *positive reframing* and is the first step towards shifting your thinking away from a pessimistic, unhappy and negative place and into a hopeful, more positive and loving space: a space where real long-lasting and positive change is possible.

STEP 3

Every time your child does something from the positive side of this list, however small, even if it's just playing nicely with their toys, or just looking at you and giving you a smile, or just handing you their plate nicely at the end of a meal, or just sitting at the table for three seconds, but really well, I want you to praise them. Imagine you have a huge bucket full of praise in the corner of every room of your house and one that you carry around. Visualize it: what does it look like – gold coins, silver dust, pink and cream hearts and stars? There's a ladle in each of your buckets, and every time you're with your child and they do something nice I want you to pour ladles of praise over your child. This is called increasing the *positive reinforcement* – seeking out the great stuff and enjoying it when it happens, plus giving it so much attention that you are shifting your child's perception of which kinds of behaviours get the best attention from you.

Let your child continue with their tantrums and try to ignore them as much as possible (more on this later), but when they're not having a tantrum smile at them, kiss and cuddle them – do things to start to increase the amount of positive interaction you have so you can see a chink of light beginning before you've even tried anything else. Just really try to shift the majority of your focus and attention from their difficult behaviour to their lovely behaviour – shift the way you are reinforcing your child's behaviour in a positive direction.

How beliefs determine behaviour – ours and our child's

Your child isn't just a problem to be solved; your child is a human being with complex and fundamental biological, emotional, psychological and social needs. They are not an inanimate object that is broken and needs fixing; they are a sensitive, receptive and intuitive individual. Therefore, if you attempt to manage their behaviour in a way that is still underpinned by exasperation and negative thoughts and feelings, they will sense this and nothing, NOTHING, will work.

To put it simply – how we THINK affects how we FEEL, which in turn affects how we BEHAVE.

Our thoughts are underpinned by our attitudes, so imagine this scenario:

You had a horrible experience at school and left with poor grades. This resulted in you also leaving with low self-esteem and a belief that you were stupid and unable to achieve. As an adult you become interested in human biology and love trying to understand the way the body works. Your friends suggest you train to be a nurse because they can see how much the subject excites you and how much you have absorbed just by watching TV programmes and reading. You send off for application forms for courses that will enable you to eventually get onto a nursing course but every time you get them out to fill them in, you break out in a cold sweat – your heart races, you shake and feel sick because you know that in truth you are conning everyone and you are actually really stupid and will fail. So why bother in the first place? You eventually bin the forms, rebuff your friends' encouragement and feel angry, unfulfilled and full of regret – emotions that you will see as further evidence of what a failure you really are.

ATTITUDE:

'I'm stupid, useless, can't learn, a failure'

Look at application forms (the trigger)

THOUGHT:

'What's the point, I can't do this, this is so hard, they'll reject me anyway'

FEELINGS:

Anxiety, anger, frustration, sadness

BEHAVIOUR:

Pour a drink, eat some food, switch on the TV, throw application forms in the bin, get cranky with friends who try to encourage you

And here is an example of how your attitude to your child can set up a similar cycle:

ATTITUDE:

'My child is a monster and I cannot control their behaviour'

You go to a birthday party and are amongst lots of small children and their parents (the trigger)

THOUGHTS:

'I know she's going to pull that child's hair/push that baby over/have a tantrum if it's not her turn/break something/wet herself/be a total nightmare . . . '

FEELINGS:

Total stress, anxiety, frustration, nausea, anger

BEHAVIOUR:

Hovering around child, anxious and tense body language, stressed and frustrated tone of voice, picking up on every negative thing your child does, nagging your child . . .

OUTCOME:

Your child picks up on your tension and fulfils the role you have set up for them thus getting a huge amount of attention. Because you are feeling out of control and stressed you do nothing effective except give your child all that negative attention for what they are doing. Hence they learn nothing and will continue with their difficult behaviour when they are with you. In contrast, if you go in feeling positive and in control, your thoughts, feelings and behaviour will allow you to manage your child in a way that is calm, cheerful and if necessary clearly assertive and so enables them to be clear about what you expect from them, and enables you to manage any problem behaviours decisively as and when necessary – which enables both of you to have fun.

So with your child the thought-feeling-behaviour cycle will work in exactly the same way and whether it enables you to feel positive or negative about your child and yourself as a parent depends on the attitudes that you hold. And in the same way that the early school experiences of our friend on page 28 led them to develop negative attitudes and a low self-esteem about their academic abilities, your early life experiences of being a child and being parented will have shaped your attitudes and self-esteem about yourself as a person and about yourself as a parent.

This is a part of a much bigger discussion and one that comes in Part Three of this book, so until then all I will say is that while it is not a given, if you've had a difficult childhood or have experiences and memories that are painful and problematic, then it is fairly logical that for some people in this situation becoming a parent may be polluted with these experiences, which will impact negatively on your attitudes to parenting and yourself as a parent.

Looking at these issues is likely to be painful, and therefore I want us to hold on to these thoughts but to put them aside for now until you are feeling more positive about your child and their behaviour. You will then feel stronger, better about yourself as a parent and in a better emotional space to reflect more deeply, and at that point we will come to a more detailed and necessary exploration of some of these core issues in Part Three (see page 140).

Until then we will just agree that your child is not responsible for what happened to you as a child or how you feel about the way you were parented and in turn how that has shaped your beliefs about yourself as a parent. Equally, our children are also not responsible for any current stresses or pressures we are under. These experiences, past and present, shape and inform your beliefs and behaviours as a parent. Thus it is vitally important that we as adults have enough insight into being able, as far as is possible, to draw a line between pressures on us from the past and the present and the totally legitimate pressures that our child places on us – the then and now. This is why I am urging you to make a huge conscious effort to shift your perception of your child and yourself as their parent into a more positive and optimistic space so that the real changes can begin.

Further positive shifts in your attitudes and beliefs

This is also a good time to introduce sticker charts if you haven't used them already in your family. Actually, I suspect that most of you have and some of you will now have your head in your hands groaning that they don't work. They do work, but only if they are done in a committed, conscientious and positive way. And let me tell you a secret – their purpose isn't to train the child to behave better – oh no! It's to train you, the parent.

I will introduce behaviour-shaping charts later in the book but right now let's start off with a really simple sticker chart where you can get your child and yourself into the notion of what it means. We are going to make a chart built around things that your child can already do.

So, if your child is a behavioural nightmare in one or many areas of their life, but does clean their teeth well, will sit at the table and eat their food nicely and put their shoes on when asked, then let's focus on that. Here's an example:

	Clean my teeth well	Sit nicely at table	Big girl shoes on	Put teddy on my bed each morning
Monday				
Tuesday				
Wednesday				
Thursday				
Friday				
Saturday				
Sunday				

If you have just read this and are thinking, Well, that's no good –
I couldn't make a sticker chart about anything: my child's too
much of a devil!, then you haven't thought hard enough and you
need to go back, reread the last section and find perhaps just the
one thing that you can see at the moment as lovely behaviour
(there are probably more good behaviours from your child and
as you work on shifting your negative attitude towards them you
will begin to see them with different eyes).

Build a chart around that one behaviour (or possibly more).
The chart will remind you to notice and positively reinforce this
behaviour. Make the chart with your child and explain to them
that each time they do the behaviour as you ask them to, they
get a sticker – which they can put in the box on the chart.

Because children are children and hence can't be expected
to always get it right, this needs to be reflected in how we reward
them and their behaviour. Also, because this is a period of
learning, we must allow them to make the odd mistake because
it is only then that they can eventually learn to correct themselves.
So, if your child gets at least three out of four of the daily stickers
(75%), then they get a small treat at the end of the day. If we
allowed them to get a treat for two out of four stickers (50%),
we are then rewarding them for behaviour that may have occurred
by chance. As your child learns, and their behaviour is shaped in
a positive direction, we can up the stakes with new behaviours
on the chart with the expectation that they do get 100% for
those behaviours they are now used to being rewarded for.

When you give the sticker for each behaviour and then the
small treat at the end of the day, do this with a huge amount of
praise and cuddles (don't use food as a reward, just something
small – in these days of rising childhood obesity we don't want
children to use food as emotional self-comfort). If your child
doesn't do as asked, which will happen because they will be
testing out this new positive parent and wondering where the
one they can make cross has gone, just take them to the chart
and in front of them draw a sad face in the box. Be very calm,

and say that maybe next time they'll get their sticker and so, therefore, their small treat.

Emphasize any praise and play down any disappointment. In doing so you are reversing the trend for your child and teaching them that there is a new system in town – one whereby they get attention for being helpful and lovely, not by being shouted at. Don't over-sticker the chart and don't let your child take control of it. When you prompt them, *only ask twice* for them to do the behaviour and make sure you communicate in a clear and understandable manner, on their level and making eye contact. By limiting yourself to only asking twice: once nicely (with eye contact and smiles) and then once firmly (with eye contact and a firm and assertive tone of voice), you stop getting into a cycle of nagging that then leads them to ignore you. You also establish a boundary, which teaches them that when their parents ask them to do something they mean business. Depending on whether they do as asked or not, be consistent in your response and then either enthusiastically reward or calmly draw in the sad face.

This process is one of the major ways we learn and it is called **operant conditioning** (or instrumental learning). If implemented effectively, this is a process in which the frequency of a response increases as a result of a reward (the reinforcement) occurring immediately after that response is carried out. Not rocket science but it's good to be aware of this as you begin to recognize how your operant conditioning of your child's behaviour might have, until now, been lodged mostly in a negative direction and therefore increased the frequency of the negative behaviours.

You see, you thought sticker charts were designed to change children's behaviour – oh no! These are a tool to train you, the parent, to praise and be positive to your child.

The kiss-cuddle game!

Alongside ladling the praise from the buckets around your home
and your simple sticker chart, also begin a process of counting
how many times you tell your child you love them or that you're
proud of them, or go up to them for a kiss and a cuddle. And a
lot of parents will say, 'Well, they never want to kiss and cuddle
me!' But would you want to kiss and cuddle anyone who you
thought was cross with you and stressed out by you all the time?

   You therefore might need to consciously make yourself go over
to your child, grab them in your arms and give them a lovely big
kiss and a cuddle, a tickle and a squeeze – make it a game. If they
struggle and are not used to this, build up slowly with very brief
cuddles. Don't take it personally or feel rejected and so give up.

   Build the kiss-cuddle game into their routine and make sure
they get at least three before they go to school, three as they get
home from school, three once they play or watch telly and have
tea, three before bath, three in the bath – and so on. You cannot
over-cuddle a child. Set up a routine for yourself as a parent and
even make a chart and tick each kiss-cuddle off if you need to
until it becomes second nature.

Play

As you monitor the quality and type of interaction you have with your child, also look at how much you play with them. Many of us spend all our time clearing up, cleaning, rush, rush, rushing about and leave the children to get on with it. If they bother us and want us to play with them (notice the word 'bother' in that sentence), we will often respond with, 'Oh look, go and play, can't you see Mummy/Daddy is busy?'

I'm not saying that you must play all the time with your children because it is also important that they learn to entertain themselves. However, play is understood by many leading experts in child development as being one of the most positive and powerful tools we have as parents. Play enables the development of social, communication, numerical and countless other life skills but, most fundamentally, play is extremely powerful in the building of strong, loving and positive parent-child bonds.

So, forget the endless tasks of the day; just get down with your child and make sure you spend at least half an hour playing a game that they initiate and absolutely do not take control of it. And when you play that game I want you to do two things: attend and reward.

Attending means watching what your child is doing, and giving a positive running commentary – imagine you are a sports commentator on the radio and you have to paint a vivid and enthusiastic picture for your listeners. So with your child you would say: 'Oh, so the car's going up the track – that's really great! Oh, it's got stuck? What are you going to do – you're going to change the tyre? Aren't you clever!'

When you say, 'Aren't you clever!' you are *rewarding* your child. The fun and happy play behaviour becomes reinforced by building a new positively powerful relationship with your child. Thus you are teaching your child that they get so much from their relationship with you that is fun and happy when they are behaving in a calm, focused and positive manner. This message will feed through to their everyday behaviour and so build up to a mutually collaborative and loving relationship for life. And apart from all the psychological theorizing you will just really love these moments as you watch your child play, listen to their chatter and enter their little world – such moments that you will increasingly make time for will really focus you on the beauty of being a parent. And don't forget to tell them: 'Come here, give me a kiss because I love playing with you, you clever sausage!' Or something like that!

Why am I asking you to do all this? Listing the qualities of your child and yourself with an emerging focus more on the positives; ladling praise; the simple sticker chart; the kiss-cuddle game; play with attendant positive commentary and rewarding hugs and kisses? By now I think you will be able to answer this question. If you're still not sure, please don't worry but do give this another go from the start because sometimes it takes time to make such significant shifts in attitudes, thinking, feelings and behaviour.

The reason I want you to start this motivational process before we even begin to think about changing behaviour is to shift the focus of the dynamic of the relationship between you the parent and your child. We have to do this for any of the techniques to work.

The problem behaviours may still exist but now you are seeing them as behaviours rather than a marker of who your child is. You are also looking beyond them to see the sweet loveable child who you couldn't live without and would throw down your life for. You've got *your* child, and fundamentally she/he's the one you want. And you look at them when they're asleep and your heart wants to burst out of your chest. Maybe you are also beginning to see that you have real value as a parent– I hope you do.

Understanding your child's behaviour and your responses – some words of caution!

Please forgive me but before we finally move on to Part Two – the 'how to' section – some final words of caution.

EXTENDED FAMILY

Often it's not just the parents who have labelled the child as the problem, but the extended family or other social groups: 'Oh that Timmy! He's an absolute pain!'

Poor Timmy! We've all been there. Imagine a party where you don't know many people and you've walked into an unfamiliar social grouping, and you feel like an outsider to a group. Because you are anxious, you get the feeling others are being offhand with you or see you in a certain way and this increases your anxiety and puts you in a defensive position. By thinking negatively and feeling anxious and defensive, your behaviour will begin to reflect this and you may then appear rather cold and stand-offish – making others less likely to approach you and hence fulfilling your belief that you are the outsider. Thus your behaviour generated via your anxious and negative beliefs sets others off to behave in a cold and off-hand manner – the self-fulfilling prophecy.

Similarly, if your child has a 'reputation' amongst most close and significant others (I include school in this), it is important that you enable these others to understand the self-fulfilling prophecy, as happened at the party described above – if you treat people with animosity and suspicion you will set them up to behave in a hostile and defensive manner towards you even if actually you and they are the loveliest people in the world.

If everyone thinks Timmy is a massive pain – he will be. Big time.

As a way of understanding how your child sees how they are perceived within the family and by others close to the family, encourage them to draw a picture of themselves with everyone in it. If they are not old enough to do this but there are other children in the family (siblings or cousins or close friends' older children), ask them to draw everyone instead and so gauge their 'outsider' perspective. Do not do anything other than sit with them and watch. Children are very perceptive and sometimes their drawings can be very revealing. Do not make any suggestions or interfere with the drawing.

If you don't think your child will do it unselfconsciously with you sitting next to them, ask a friend to do it with them while you hover unobtrusively in the background and then look at the drawings afterwards.

- Who do they draw and in what order?
- What size is each person compared to the others?
- Where do they place each person in relation to others and themselves?
- Who is near each other, who seems marginalized and on the edges?
- Does your child feel close to or alienated from you?
- Are their siblings between you and them?
- Are they part of the main group or on the edge?
- What are the facial expressions of those they have drawn – who do they think are happy, who are sad?

Don't get too overly anxious about this – just use whatever you see as another way of thinking about your child's role in the family, how they are perceived and how they see this from their point of view. This is a way in which your child can communicate their own perspective on the issues we are thinking about in an unselfconscious manner. Children notice more than we give them credit for and they are telling us so much about our behaviour because they are little emotional barometers of what's going on in the family. So, for children of the age we are thinking about, communication about how they feel is predominantly via their actions – whether that be drawings, tantrums or a refusal to eat, rather than via their still-developing words and sentences.

If you are attempting to change your behaviour, and consequently your child's behaviour, in a more positive direction, it is vital that you share this process with those who also have significant contact with your child – particularly anyone who co-parents with you or is involved in their care. Children need consistent messages in order to understand where they stand and what is expected of them. So, if possible, share the philosophies and ideas we've thought about, that are making a positive difference already, with those significantly attached to and involved with your child.

What is a toddler?

At this point in our process, as we are really examining how we and others close to us perceive our child, I think it is important to actually focus on where your child is developmentally. While there can be no doubt that the behaviour of a young child can be challenging in the extreme at times, how often do we get angry with our children about things they do that are actually less to do with them being 'bad' or 'naughty' and more a reflection of the stage of development that they currently inhabit?

There is some disagreement about the age range of the toddler. Some suggest between the years of one and three – to coincide (at around twelve months) with the beginning of rapid motor behavioural changes in many children: the onset of an early walking style that is described by the word 'toddle'. However, others ascribe the onset of the toddler years with more of the personality-based behavioural changes as the young child becomes more vocal and independent in their nature – usually beginning around the age of two years and up until five years of age.

In my experience it is best not to get too hung up on describing one's child via their achievement of developmental milestones (my daughter walked at thirteen months, my son 'bum-shuffled' until nineteen months – was he a toddler later? Is that relevant?), however, it is at this stage of development that many parents feel a sudden urge to label their child and their development in a way that can become slightly neurotic and at times competitive with their friends and their children.

The word toddler also seems to be used by some as a health-and-safety warning as sometimes parents will describe their child as a toddler with a groan, a sigh and a sense of 'watch out' here comes trouble. We also have the label the 'terrible twos', which is used to describe the sometimes ferocious tantrums that come with being a toddler at around the age of two years. Bear in mind the negative qualities associated with the word toddler as you continue to think about how your attitudes and beliefs towards your child and their behaviour will directly impact on the behaviour produced.

Developmentally, toddlerhood is a demanding and exciting, exhausting and challenging time – both for you as the parent and also the little mite going through it all. And, in order for you to help your child through these times without becoming overwhelmed by the new behavioural challenges you are suddenly dealing with, it is important to take some time to reflect on why your child, who you are finding a struggle, is the way they are. In an ideal world, the most effective parent would be one that is able to step back from their child's behaviour, trying to deal with it rationally and calmly rather than emotionally. Of course we do not live in an ideal world and often we are dealing with many competing demands and pressures on our time and our emotions. However, it is worth remembering the obvious – that as we become stressed, exasperated and emotional with our children, we (the adult in the relationship) will inevitably end up inhabiting the same cross, stressed and tantrum-laden space and therefore achieve nothing more than reinforcing the behaviour by role-modelling it ourselves. Developmentally, we are at a stage of our life that enables us to think through and manage our feelings responsibly even when we are faced with a little person who in that moment clearly can't.

So, what are toddlers going through?

The fundamental process that occurs during the toddler years is one of separation, where your child begins to develop and utilize more independence across all areas of their physical and behavioural functioning. Motor skills develop rapidly: at around the age of one year, moving towards eighteen months, many children begin to stand, move and eventually walk unaided; they will attempt to self-feed and drink (and so your washing loads increase!) and start to manipulate toys in a more meaningful way (including a love of posting bricks into video and DVD recorders, hiding the car keys, etc.). Between eighteen months and two years of age, in the motor-skills department, most children will be walking alone and showing rapid and increasing motor-skill development via play and scribbling. Heart stoppingly, they also begin to run and climb (where did that easy-to-manage plonk-them-anywhere baby go?), particularly when on a busy street or near a flight of steep concrete steps. Between the ages of two and three years they really are zooming around and diving off the sideboard. Possessing both well-developed gross motor skills (e.g. those used when running) and fine motor skills (e.g. those used when drawing), they love nothing more than throwing the ball around in the house (especially good fun when aimed at things that make a wonderful crashing noise when hit), ramming their dolly baby buggy into the newly glossed skirting boards and taking anything apart, including batteries out of remote controls and the stitching from teddy's back. Oh and they also adore sticking things into plug sockets, especially their fingers.

So, from the point of view of helping them along with their motor-skill development you need to: gaffer tape them in bubble wrap, grow swivelling eyes (with night vision) in the back and sides of your head, increase your sprinting and tackling speeds and disconnect all electricity sources coming into your home.

As these motor skills develop there is also a certain amount of frustration that accompanies the process – I'm talking about theirs here, not yours! This is because the associated cognitive development can sometimes be at odds with what is going on in the motor department and so dolly gets chucked across the room as your previously nicely playing little one dissolves into Oscar-winning tears because she knew she wanted dolly to wear her dress but couldn't quite manage to get it on. Intent not realized by actual achievement equals enormous anger and frustration – a tantrum.

Another amazing mental development can be witnessed with the onset of language, which develops rapidly from around five words at about twelve months, doubling to about twenty words at eighteen months. From then on there is a huge upsurge in number of words used (between twenty and fifty), the way they are beginning to be put together and also the comprehension of language heard. Now they are at the age of between two and three years, word acquisition is rapid and the words are used imaginatively and in sentences. Alongside speech and language developments we see play developing from early brick stacking at eighteen months to more imaginative side-by-side play at three years, and more group friendship play developing from three onwards. Play at two begins to involve sorting and stacking and takes on another meaning as our child grasps causal action relationships such as pressing a button to switch on a light or play a tune (this is the moment when toys become sound-and-vision torture after a computerized nursery rhyme has bombarded your brain for fifteen minutes). At the age of two your child will also begin to use trial-and-error strategies for learning (showing the early development of problem solving).

Moving from two to three, cognitive development really comes into its own as it begins to merge with motor-skill development and behaviour. By now your child enjoys routines, has an imagination, sings, dances, knows how to pull faces or break wind to make people laugh and generally becomes their own one-person show. As you observe your child at this magical time also notice how they have more will and intent attached to what they do as they recognize that they can get responses from others via their behaviour and so play for attention – the laughs, the cuddles and also the shouting.

How a toddler thinks

At this point it is also worth examining how your child's ability to process information will have a huge impact on their behaviour. Under the age of three years old, your child will not have fully developed the brain structures that are involved in the understanding of their behaviour and the processing of information about their behaviour (mainly located in the frontal lobes of the brain). Many of us, however, treat our child as if they can process and understand this information and so parent our children via lengthy explanations about what they have done, why they shouldn't and what we want them to do differently. Given that children are so linguistically adept and can produce phrases that sound extremely intelligent and well thought out (mostly picked up from the television), we are seduced into believing that our little one is actually taking our discussions on board. But, given their stage of frontal-lobe development, they're not. Therefore, by talking to our children what we are actually doing is giving them huge attention for what they've done (they have got our time and full attention as we chat away to them) and so we are actually reinforcing the behaviour when we are trying to get it to stop! For young children actions speak louder than words – clear instructions and consistent consequences for undesirable behaviour works – lengthy discussions don't.

Also, before we really focus on the behavioural development of the toddler, it is useful to consider another fundamental cognitive change that occurs at around one year: *object permanence*. This important shift in perception is evident when our child suddenly learns that although they can't see an object (e.g. a ball that has rolled behind a sofa) it does still exist and they can go and look for it. However, having mastered object permanence our two-year-old will still show the endearing narcissism they have when they run into a room shouting, 'She's coming!' with the expectation that because they know who *she* is, we all will too. Another example of this perceptual narcissism is when they close their eyes and believe, because they can't see us, that we also can't see them. By considering these cognitive changes we can also understand some of the key personality-based behavioural changes that are taking place and underpin your reasons for reading this book – behaviours that fundamentally revolve around the use of the word 'NO!'.

Classic toddler behaviour

I hope that you've got to this part and just want to throw this book down and scream. I hope that you are feeling frustrated and bogged down with the explanations and occasional use of jargon. I hope that as you read my rather pared-down list of a few key aspects of toddler development you felt the words swim before your eyes – not because I want to appear the expert, but because I want to engender in you some of what it must feel like at times to be the little person going through it all. It feels overwhelming, bewildering, frustrating, exhausting and at times nonsensical. That's right – it's not easy being a toddler, especially because they haven't even got all the cognitive skills to explain or comprehend why they are feeling the way they are.

So, yes, by the age of twelve to eighteen months (for some of you maybe earlier) your child:

1

Will have temper tantrums – they are physically and mentally exhausted; they don't understand what is going on; they just want to get teddy's trousers on but can't; their brother has taken the green brick they wanted but they haven't the verbal skills to tell him nor the social skills to understand that bashing him over the head with the red brick isn't very nice; they have just been landed with a new sibling.

2

Will only say the word 'NO!' – they are tired; they are beginning to recognize the way they can affect your behaviour; they live in a narcissistic world labelled ME because they still have to learn some of the fundamental social skills of living; they learn that if they hold out long enough they can either get a fantastic reaction from us or their own way; they have just been landed with a new sibling.

3

May hit and/or bite – they are tired; they don't know how to say 'excuse me but I think you'll find I was playing with that train first'; they feel stressed and anxious (the fight/flight response) and so revert to the fight mode and get rid of their stress and anger and frustration via their teeth into someone else's leg; they have just been landed with a new sibling.

4

May be clingy – they are experiencing separation anxiety; they are going through a normal toddler stage of neophobia: the fear of new experiences (people/situations/food/etc.); they have just been landed with a new sibling.

5

May refuse to eat/sleep in their bed/ use the potty – all of the above. Your child is having their unique reaction to the most physically, mentally and emotionally exhausting period of development at a time of life when the skills they need to understand and communicate how they are feeling are the skills that are actually in the process of development.

Your child is behaving like a toddler because they are a toddler.

The reason their behaviour has now become problematic to you is because (and please forgive me for being blunt) you have done one, several or all of the following:

1

Given them too much attention for their normal toddler behaviour and so reinforced it and taught them as they are learning to become independent that their difficult behaviour gets the most attention from you.

2

Become panicked and stressed by their tantrums/biting/anxiety/faddy eating (because you've felt judged by others or have compared your child to others) and so dealt with it in a way that panics your child and makes their behaviour more likely to reoccur.

3

Held unrealistic expectations of their behaviour and so overreacted to developmentally normal toddler behaviour.

4

Expected them to have a level of cognitive and behavioural control that they just don't have yet, and so have become frustrated when they don't really understand your explanations to them about their behaviour, and when they can't do what you want as quickly as you want.

5

Had another baby/babies and have elevated your toddler into the role of the older sibling and so forgotten their developmental needs and also how their behaviour may reflect how they are feeling about having a sibling.

6

You also lead a busy life with a number of life stresses. You want to do the best but sometimes feel overwhelmed. Somehow everybody else seems to manage their kids/life/everything better than you. You're mentally and physically exhausted.

So, here's the thing. Your child is going through an extremely challenging time of major biological, social, emotional and psychological development, a time that is key to them separating from you and becoming more independent self-functioning beings. This stage of development exhausts, frustrates and bewilders them and they will show these feelings in a predominantly behavioural way because they don't have the cognitive and verbal abilities to comprehend and explain what they are feeling. This is all entirely normal.

You are going through an extremely challenging time of biological, social, emotional and psychological change. You have a number of responsibilities that can and do at times overwhelm you. Although the grown up, sometimes you don't feel like one and want to drop to the floor in a tantrum, releasing rage and sobs. You love your child more than anything but when you are stressed and tired find their behaviour impossible to cope with. You think that you are doing a bad job as a parent and so feel anxious and stressed. This is all entirely normal.

But you now want to change some of these difficulties. You want to feel more positive about yourself as a parent and your child as a child. You want to feel more calm and in control, less phased by behaviour that you now realize is understandable given what your child is going through, and entirely normal.

You are now ready to start a positive and enthusiastic process of change. Well, almost ready – just got to get you really understanding your anxiety and stress so that it doesn't pollute all your positive and good intentions.

Anxiety

The anxiety response is called the 'fight or flight' syndrome and it's a primitive inbuilt response to threat. So, if we feel threatened, we will either fight what is making us feel threatened or run away from it. And that could be something external, as in a person or thing, or it could be internal – a memory.

Having a child brings anxiety from the minute you hold them in your arms for the first time and you suddenly realize that you are responsible for keeping them alive. If that anxiety builds, and as the parenting challenges become greater over time we cannot manage it, we will enter the fight or flight mode and either yell at our child or withdraw from them. If we project our anxiety onto our child, they will in turn feel threatened or stressed.

Like us, children will also show a fight or flight response because they are frustrated, stressed or anxious. So you may get children who are aggressive, and who get cross and angry very quickly (the fight response). Or you may get children who, at the dinner table will refuse to eat food, because they can sense the maternal or paternal anxiety around feeding time and so they will respond to food in a way that is both avoidant and withdrawing (the flight response). In both instances they are responding to the anxiety that they are feeling in the atmosphere. The differences in their reactions come from differing personalities that arise out of the genetic and environmental mix that influences all personality and development.

Your anxiety and stress might manifest itself as neurotic overblown hysteria – big shouting and hair tearing. However, some of you may not fight straight back at your child and go over the top emotionally, but you may withdraw and disconnect from your child completely – ignoring them, maybe sitting on the sofa and watching telly, and it's only when your child does something that you look over and scream at them. In each instance it's the same set of responses: either an immediate reaction directly at the threat or a withdrawal from it, possibly responding later.

So, I've either met parents who are anxious and constantly reinforcing this behaviour negatively by giving attention at the times when their child is doing what they don't want them to do, or parents who are so withdrawn from the child that the child is then doing anything to get their attention because there is nothing being given to them. Thus one parent is overanxious and overbearing in their responses, and the other parent is withdrawn with a 'let them get on with it' style.

The anxiety response

A useful approach to managing our stress and anxiety responses comes from understanding what is happening to us (biologically, cognitively and behaviourally) at these moments and how it impacts on our behaviour. When we are confronted by a situation or a person who we experience as a stressor or threat, we experience a series of physiological changes that enable us to deal with that threat and ensure our survival – this primitive inbuilt response enables our body to fight that threat or run away from it. The sympathetic division of the autonomic nervous system is activated via activity in the hypothalamus and the pituitary and adrenal glands of the brain. There is the release of acetylcholine, which leads to the release of the hormones epinephrine (adrenaline) and norepinephrine. Following this, our bodies will have physical responses that are designed to prepare us most efficiently to fight or run – our heart and breathing rate increase (to increase oxygenated blood supply and delivery), the blood vessels to the muscles dilate (most needed to run and fight), our pupils dilate, we sweat (to keep ourselves cool), our digestive actions cease (we are not going to eat at this moment in time) and our bladder and bowels relax (so we can dump any additional load and therefore flee faster). Our body is primed for survival, which is a basic biological and physiological function, therefore our thinking becomes more black and white (there is no grey abstract area when it comes to survival) and our focus is purely on the object(s) of fear – hence our perceptions become exaggerated and magnified, our thinking and behaviour concrete and disinhibited.

Now in the case of an early hunting scenario where we are out in the wilds trying to kill tonight's supper this fight or flight survival mechanism is of course vital in order for us to react to danger and survive. However, in today's society where our stresses are so different (e.g. our child having a tantrum in public) we are extremely disadvantaged by the fact that we have not evolved away from the fight/flight response because we need responses that enable us to face our fear in a calm and rational way, not in an instinctive biological and physical way.

Translating all this into our experience as parents in times of stress, when our child is behaving in a way that makes us feel threatened and out of control, we will feel muscle tension and our heart will race, our breathing will quicken and we might experience tightening of the chest and cramps in our stomach – all these physiological signs tell you that there is something to fear and also cause you to become a more primitive biological organism rather than one that can think and rationalize abstractly and logically. If you think about it, this makes complete sense because in a primitive survival scenario the last thing we need to do is stop and think; what we need is the ability to react and do so fast.

And so when we consider the anxiety that comes with parenting, plus additional stresses and tensions that we may be coping with in our lives, we will enter the same primitive response pattern and thus lose the ability to think and parent clearly and confidently, and start shouting and yelling (fight) or withdraw and give in (flight).

Anxiety management and successful parenting

As we go through each of the technique sections, what I really want you to think about is how the stress and anxiety that currently exists in whatever problem you are trying to deal with is intrinsically part of the problem and, as hard as it will be, you have to find a way to step back, relax and get a real handle on your perception of the problem if you are going to solve it. Because the fundamental truth is that if you come at any kind of problem with a set of techniques and full of good intentions, but still gripped by anxiety, then you will fail.

A state of anxiety and long-term stress about your child's behaviour (because they are out of control/because they're not sleeping/because they wet themselves all the time/because they don't eat…) will lead you to feel very anxious and self-doubting as a parent, and feel out of control and powerless in the face of your child's behaviour. You might have great concerns and fears that your child and indeed yourself are being judged by other people and so that will have built up into a huge ball of anxiety and stress, causing you to lie awake at night worrying about your child. This of course has led you to develop a negative mindset about them, which then compounds and perpetuates the anxiety – and in turn compounds and maintains the problem behaviours.

Your child has behavioural difficulties because, despite these probably being very developmentally appropriate behaviours, they were perceived by you as socially unacceptable and embarrassing, and so you built those issues into big problems and became stressed and anxious about them: that stress and anxiety will then have compounded the behaviour of your child – and so you get this circular, self-fulfilling cycle.

Here's an example I have met many times in my clinical years:

- The child isn't sleeping through the night.
- The parents are exhausted and life has no colour in it; they can't enjoy themselves; they're yelling at everyone; they and their partner haven't had any intimate time together for months or maybe years because they're too exhausted or their child is in their bed.
- This one problem has a trickle-down effect and suddenly the marriage is looking a bit shaky; relationships with friends are looking a bit shaky because the parents can never go out any more because they're so incredibly tired all the time; the other kids are suffering because the parents are yelling at them; the parents have put on weight and they just feel so unattractive but are too exhausted to exercise and just eat to keep themselves going . . .
- Suddenly one thing becomes a huge number of things: stress leads to anxiety, which changes our behaviour, and so we make the problem worse.

But just having an understanding, a conceptualization of why you're in this place, and giving yourself a break and then starting to realize that there is a solution somewhere down the line, takes away so much anxiety that I promise you will suddenly find that your child's behaviour starts to change before you've even done anything specific.

Really consider how you can use what we've thought about so far as a way of normalizing your anxieties and fears and associated negative beliefs about your child and yourself; reduce the stress and tension, reduce the atmosphere and behaviour that will set your child off. As you become more realistic about the problems that have led you to buy this book, also be realistic about the fact that you won't be able to resolve everything because life and all it throws at us isn't going to allow that.

And nor should it – life is about learning to tolerate as well as to change, to weather storms rather than expecting to live only in fair weather.

Finally, before we move on to the part where you can learn how to create the Von Trapp children (no thank you!), consider this: when your child is eighteen how necessary was it to be so anxious, so uptight about the whole parenting thing and not to have enjoyed it more? Now you're freaking because your child is difficult to toilet train but how many sixteen-year-olds do you see walking around in a nappy? I mean, you just don't; the process will happen, but the more you feed the anxiety, via your fight or flight behaviour, the more your child will withdraw and go pee behind the sofa or poo in their pants in the garden shed, or they'll fight you and have a massive tantrum.

So, please: chill. Chill, chill, chill, as much as you can.

I might as well be honest with you now and say that none of the techniques you read below will be any different from what you've read and tried before, but the manner in which you approach them will now be significantly different, and that is why you and your child will have a positive experience. Anyone can write a book about the techniques of parenting – it's simple behaviourism plus a lot of common sense – but as a clinical psychologist I know the real skill isn't in teaching the right way to do things, but enabling each family to make those approaches their own and really address the key issues that lie below the surface.

This part of the book is purely about specific problems and associated techniques. The reason it comes now is because I think it would be foolish of me not to enable you to start to make changes, now that you have a more positive approach and an understanding of how you have been part of the problem behaviours. Also, I know if I took you first into a discussion about what the underlying issues might be you would probably throw this book away as you need to see some changes and haven't the emotional energy to explore deeper at the moment. Fair enough – let's begin to make those changes but let me say very clearly now – if you do well in this section and then stop reading the book, any solutions that have been reached will be undone. So here's the deal: we begin the process of behaviour change here (your behaviour and your child's behaviour) and then, when you are feeling more positive about how things are going, look at the deeper issues in order to ensure the changes you have made are maintained.

As discussed so far, before looking at any issues individually the key question to ask is – why do we as parents find these behaviours so difficult to deal with or manage? It's partly about control: we lead lives where things have to be done quickly because there is so much we need to do and there aren't enough hours in the day. It's also about our anxieties: are we doing it 'right'? Are these behaviours telling us something about our child's personality? What do other people think? And it's also that these behaviours are extremely draining, especially when we lead such busy lives. They can have a significant impact on the functioning of a family, the happiness of a family and the running of a day. I've worked with families where they are literally housebound because of the child's behaviour, and this has such an impact on the whole of the family function that other problems then start, like a snowball rolling down the hill.

Ultimately, when tackling behaviour problems, you need to look at things from two perspectives. The first is behaviourally, where you ask, 'What am I doing to reinforce the behaviour that I'm seeing? Is my response causing this behaviour to become out of control?' These questions will be answered by your implementation of the behavioural techniques outlined in this section.

The second perspective is where you ask, '*Why* is my child behaving in this way?' This is a question about what else is going on in your and your child's life and we will explore it more in Part Three. This question is less vital as we tackle behaviour change, but extremely important once you have made the positive changes and want to maintain them. Sometimes children behave 'badly' for all sorts of reasons and sometimes because they are responding to the emotional temperature of the family, and there's something more going on. Children are little barometers and it's important to recognize that there are often children whose behaviour is a reflection of bigger problems within the family system. Their behaviour might be saying something that they can't verbalize, that things aren't good; things feel bad.

We are looking at your child's behaviour from both perspectives: (1) what is the behaviour and what am I doing to reinforce that behaviour? And (2) the deeper underlying question – why this behaviour is occurring – which we will address later.

So far we have discussed how motivation affects outcome – do you really want change? Are you really prepared to look at yourself in all of this? We've thought about how your (and others') attitudes towards your child and towards yourself as a parent are fundamentally linked to both the problems you are experiencing and whether you will achieve a positive solution. We've understood the behavioural model that explains how we reinforce behaviour – the behaviour that gets the most attention will happen the most often. This is also true if your child gets mostly negative attention (i.e., for when they are behaving badly) and less attention at other more positive times: they will play up for whatever attention they can get and will continue to use that behaviour if they can see it works in getting your focus on them.

Positive reinforcement is the way forward even now when you are still finding your child and their behaviour difficult. For them to respond positively to you with love and respect you must first show them those responses whenever you can. We've thought about using a simple sticker chart to help the beginning of this process. We've discussed the importance of play as a powerful parenting tool not only for child development but also for developing a strong parent-child bond. We also considered how non-verbal communication is sometimes more potent in our interactions with our children than our verbal behaviour. And, finally, we reminded ourselves that your child, as a toddler and beyond, has entered a stage of development where they will show a myriad behaviours that will be challenging but that is where they should be – they have a developmental right to behave like a child. You, on the other hand, as their parent, don't!

Having taken all that on board and started some positive shifts in your relationship and interactions with your child, what next? Well, my advice is to take it in stages.

Analysing and understanding what is going on

KEEP A DIARY

At the back of the book there is a simple diary you can use. This is called an 'ABC diary', which stands for Antecedent, Behaviour, Consequence. The antecedent is the trigger: what triggered off your child's behaviour. The behaviour section is for a description of what they did. And finally the consequence column is for you to describe your behaviour – what you did in response. Every time there is an incidence of behaviour that you're not happy with, write down in the columns where you were, what the time was, what happened, what your child did, what you did and the eventual outcome. Keep it for a minimum of a week, and then look for any patterns that show how your responses are impacting on your child. I'll show you how to do this on page 68.

By breaking down your child's behaviour and your own responses in this simple way, you will discover some very helpful information, for example whether there is a particular time of day that your child behaves in a certain way and not at other times, or whether there is a specific set of situations in which your child exhibits a particular behaviour, or whether there is a type of behaviour that tends to crop up more than others. You can also see very clearly how your response to your child's behaviour is likely to be an important key to it continuing.

Alongside noting down periods of difficult behaviour, keep a log of the amount of time that you praise your child, the moments when you have had a positive response to your child's positive behaviours. You may find yourself caught in the trap of spending more time responding to the behaviour that you don't like, which takes us back to the behavioural model: the more you respond to a particular behaviour, the more you will see that behaviour, even if the response is negative. In your child's eyes any big response is fuss and attention against times when there is very little.

The fascinating thing about self-monitoring through the diary is that as soon as you start this process you may find that the behaviour starts to shift. Because as soon as you become *aware* of how you respond, or take note of the trigger for a particular behaviour, you will probably make a subtle but effective change almost immediately. Often parents come back to me and say, 'Just by keeping the diary I'm finding that things are feeling a lot easier.' And that's because they're probably behaving slightly differently to their child, because they can see what they're doing, but also because the diary allows you to break it up in a way that feels more manageable rather than this hysterical anxious mess of 'I can't cope; my child's out of control'.

2 REVERSE THE TREND

The next step is to really think about the behaviour in terms of how you and others are reinforcing it. If you can see that every time your child begins to tantrum you charge in there with all guns blazing (thus giving it a huge amount of attention), or, when they wake fifteen times a night you are reinforcing the behaviour by giving cuddles or drinks or making night-time playtime, or you are having long and involved conversations about behaviour with a little brain that can't process the content but loves the attention that the chat is giving – then the first thing to do is to try to take a step back, say and do nothing and just try to ignore what you don't like.

The flip side of this then is to praise your child when they are being lovely. Parents can really complicate the notion of praising their child but it means nothing more than loving your child. Parents will ask me, 'How many times a day should I kiss and hug my child?' and my answer is, 'Why do you need to ask that question?' If you walk into a room and they're sitting quietly but they just look gorgeous, kiss them.

Try to put a boundary round the periods of bad behaviour so that you can move more easily into periods where you reinforce your child's good behaviour. If, for example, one of your daughters has hit her younger sister, you deal with it there and then (see next few pages for more on this), and – going back to the diary headings – you respond in a very decisive manner with a clear consequence that is consistent and that is followed through. Then an hour later when they are behaving well you don't need to withhold cuddles or praise because of the earlier behaviour. As soon as the behaviour and your response to it is over, you can move on as if nothing has happened. The mistake a lot of parents make is that the child has done X and then the parent will keep that going throughout the whole day – almost like bearing a grudge. Well, hold on a minute! Aren't children children? Isn't it in their job description to play up, test out the boundaries? Aren't they in the developmental phase of learning about behavioural self-control, social and communication skills? Aren't you therefore holding a grudge against your child for being ... *a child*?

Picture it from your child's point of view: they are having a tantrum, we ignore them and they get no attention. Then twenty minutes later they stop having a tantrum when they realize they're not getting any attention. Later they do something really lovely and we then kiss and cuddle them – somewhere in their little brain there is going to be a message along the lines of 'well, this is much nicer; this is what I want', so then they will start to work towards the good attention and work away from the behaviour that gets them nowhere at all.

Remember they are children, and they will forever more have their 'moments'! We're not designing little compliant Von Trapp children here – all scrubbed, shiny faced and saccharine never-ending sweetness. Nope!

The basic behavioural notion, therefore, is that to extinguish the behaviour you don't want, you do not reinforce it. And that cuts across all areas, from sleep problems to fussy eating. Using sleep as an example, if every time your child wakes in the night you pick them up, cuddle them, kiss them, rock them, sing them a song and give them a bottle of milk, then they're going to wake up for that every night, because it's exciting and it's lots of attention. It's unfair on your child to expect anything else.

So, first of all, monitor yourself. Secondly, if you are dealing with a situation where there are no issues of safety then just very simply try to ignore what you don't like, and praise what you do like. If, however, your child's behaviour is becoming extreme or aggressive and ignoring is not appropriate then read on for alternative techniques.

And now (and I feel there should be a drum roll here), we are ready to begin the what-to-do section.

BEHAVIOUR

The behavioural problems that I am seeing most often are: aggression, tantrums, defiance and non-compliance.

These behaviours can be very difficult to weather and can have a huge impact on everyone's day. However, these are also behaviours that are common to young children and part of their development.

As we've discussed earlier, your child is at a stage of development where they are recognizing their own possibilities for independence and imposing their will on others. They are now roaming further away from you and exploring this big and exciting world; developing relationships and having to learn vital social skills like sharing; rapidly developing their speech and language and using words to get what they want. This is an exciting, rapid and fundamental stage of their development into little individuals.

It is also exhausting – and I'm not talking about for you as the parent, I mean for them. Each day they are growing, observing, thinking, reasoning, talking, running, playing – soaking up every experience they can. So, like you, when they are exhausted they can become grumpy and non-compliant. Also they will have many experiences where they know what they want to do but can't – they will feel frustrated and get cross as their motor skills aren't up to executing the task they are attempting. So they will tantrum. Finally, they are beginning to recognize that they can't always have what they want, when they want, and this is going to be very upsetting. For many children of your child's age they are likely also to be joined by a new sibling and that can be a real blow and cause much cross foot-stamping behaviour.

Are these children therefore being 'naughty'? Well, maybe they are, maybe they're not, but to me that's beside the point. What they are being is exactly as they should be at their age and stage of development. Then add to this the possibility that you might not be feeling too good in yourself or maybe there are stresses in the family or possibly a myriad other reasons that make you more inclined to give your child more attention for the difficult behaviours than for the positive ones. You feel overwhelmed by their behaviour – and then the behaviours themselves get worse.

Preparing for change

Now that you have kept your diary and are clearer about what is going on in the interactions between yourself and your child, plus you are feeling more positive towards your child, you are ready to employ some techniques. But, just before we start, take a few moments to make two lists:

1 List all the lovely behaviours in your child that you want to increase via praise and encouragement.
2 List all the difficult behaviours that you want to decrease.

Make sure the lists are balanced and if you are parenting as a couple each make your own lists and then compare and agree one list from you both. These lists are beginning to define the boundaries that you as a parent wish to have in order to enable your little one to grow and develop their communication and social skills and abilities; they will also enable you to learn healthy behaviour management.

Agreed boundaries in any relationship are important as they enable all parties to feel safe and respected and to know where they stand. For children this is vitally important and just as important is that all involved in their upbringing are working from the same sheet. Therefore, define your boundaries, focus your attention positively on shaping your child's behaviour and make sure that from now on all messages your child gets are consistent – not just from you but also from others.

If you are negative in your attitude towards yourself and your child, have poor boundaries in terms of what you expect from your child and their behaviour, and there are other people who have different views and approaches with your child, then none of what I suggest in the rest of this book will work. However, if you feel positive, motivated and in total love with your child despite the problem behaviours, if you are clear about what you want to change and it is agreed with others who share the nurturing of your child – read on.

However, a huge final note of caution. It has been my experience over many years of working with families that children's behaviour will often get worse before it gets better once new boundaries are set in place as, quite understandably, they will kick against these in order to get back to what was familiar. Once you start, do not give up after a few days and slide back into being negative and despondent because then the old patterns of behaviour (yours and your child's) will return. So be prepared for this.

Managing tantrums

Tantrums can take many forms and are triggered off in a variety of ways – your child's tantrum behaviour will be unique to them. I generally advocate two distinct approaches for tantrums depending on whether they are the longer-term whingy, whiney kind of tantrum or whether they are aggressive. I will explain more in a while but first ask you to look back at your monitoring diary (that you have kept for a minimum of a week) and answer a few questions:

- Is there a specific time of day that the tantrums occur?
- Are there predictable triggers to the tantrums?
- Are there different types of tantrums depending on the situation (and so they need to be handled differently)?
- What is your response or variety of responses to the tantrums?
- How do your responses impact on the outcome of the situation?

The answers to these questions can be found in the ABC Diary below.

Day

Time	
Antecedent (What triggered the behaviour e.g. Where are you? Who are you with?)	
Behaviour (What is happening? What did your child do?)	
Consequence (How did you respond? What did you do?)	
Outcome	

DAY, DATE AND TIME

Information here will tell you :

whether there are any specific times of day when your child has
most problems; and ·

whether a lack of routine is a factor in the problems.

WHAT TRIGGERED THE BEHAVIOUR?

Information here will tell you whether there are any:

situations,

people,

places and/or

events

that can trigger off your child's difficult behaviour.

WHAT IS HAPPENING? WHAT DID YOUR CHILD DO?

**Information here will tell you exactly what your child does.
Tie it into the previous columns to see whether there are
different behaviours shown at:**

different times,

different places and/or

with different people.

Start thinking about what you are seeing and why.

HOW DID YOU RESPOND? WHAT DID YOU DO?

**Information here will tell you exactly how you are reinforcing
your child's behaviour:**

What are you doing to make your child likely to continue their
difficult behaviour?

Are you giving them inconsistent messages?

OUTCOME

**Information here will tie everything together and help you make
sense of your child's individual reactions to their world.**

Now begin to think how you can make changes to timing, triggers and your
reactions to positively impact on your child's behaviour and the outcome.

TIMING

Starting simply, it is probably useful to just examine the time-of-day column in your diary and see whether there are any changes you can make to your child's routines that would in fact have a huge and positive influence on their behaviour. How well defined are their feeding and sleeping routines? Are they sleeping enough? Do you often drag them out when they are tired and hungry and so increase the chances of their behaviour going into meltdown? Sometimes subtle changes to the daily schedule can have an enormous impact on a child's behaviour.

DISTRACTION

Moving to the next diary columns, you may begin to see a pattern of events or situations that trigger off the most difficult behaviours. And so, if you find that your child's tantrums are triggered predictably and actually now you've monitored their behaviour you can see them coming, then try to head them off at the pass by distracting your child before they lose it. Be creative: use songs, games or even point to an imaginary and ridiculous creature that, apparently, is in the garden! 'Oh look! What's that going past?' or 'Goodness me! Did you see this?' or 'Let's sing a song.' It could be anything you like, but can be a very effective way to stop a tantrum before it even starts. Amuse yourself while distracting them and then keep them going until whatever it was that would trigger them off has passed on by.

Distraction techniques are also really effective when you can see your child is bored and likely to start misbehaving, such as in restaurants, supermarkets or on a long car journey. For these times think ahead and use all your creative parenting energy to engage your child and distract them from the boredom – songs, stories and games will all help get you and your child through a dull shopping trip in no time!

IGNORE IT

If your child's tantrum is already going and even a spot of tap

dancing whilst juggling won't shift it, then it's time to get tough.
Ignoring is very powerful because a lack of attention (i.e., no
reinforcement) will mean that in time the behaviour will fade.
Tantrums are best *ignored*. Even if your child is screaming their
head off for twenty minutes on the floor, just make sure they're
safe, and walk away. If they come up and grab at you, turn round,
get down on their level, make eye contact and say, 'When you stop
screaming, I will talk to you,' and you walk away again, and then,
if necessary, you say it again clearly. But always *keep your voice
calm*, so there's very little reinforcement.

If, as you are ignoring what your child is doing, you find that
you're getting more and more wound up, just reflect on why that
is. Your child is purely having a tantrum: it's anger and rage and
it's behaviour you need to help them learn to manage. So, how
do you manage yourself and your behaviour so you don't end
up having a tantrum back at your child? Well, think about ways
in which *you can distract yourself* from what's going on – singing
Abba songs in my head was always a very helpful distraction
for me in such moments! Try to create a bit of mental distance,
so that you don't allow the behaviour to get inside you because
otherwise you will then start to react angrily to your child, thus
creating that negative cycle of behaviour.

EFFECTIVE COMMUNICATION

I recommend that parents keep ignoring their child until the
tantrum blows itself out, however, for some of you this might be
very difficult and, if so, then I suggest that you consider imposing
a consequence. This means getting down on your child's level and
telling them to stop the behaviour twice: in a tone that is first nice
and then the second time sounding more firm. Remember the
rule is: *once nicely and then once firmly*. In other words, you
can only give two commands before you impose a consequence
if your child has not done as you have asked.

This is an important rule for you as a parent because it enables
your child to learn, over time, to respond to your verbal

command themselves, and eventually they will not need any consequence to be imposed. If they don't stop the tantrum, they are told that they will lose their favourite toy. In this scenario you would then put a favourite toy on a high shelf, where they can see it, in order to show your child that their behaviour has a negative consequence. You'd then have to ignore the ensuing tantrum until they have a period of lovely behaviour and they get their toy back with a clear and brief explanation why. In this way your child is learning an important lesson for life – do unto others as you would have done to yourself!

By only asking twice you reduce the possibility that your child will just ignore you (which they will do if you nag them repeatedly) or become desensitized to your authority (which will happen if you shout at them). Also, if you are a parent who spends a lot of time chatting with your child about their behaviour rather than being clear about what you want, you will just be making their behaviour more, not less, likely to continue. All this relates to the frontal lobe development of a young child (as discussed in Part One, page 45), which means that brief authoritative words and clear actions are the most effective means of communication with a young child.

TIME OUT (ONLY FOR THE OVER-TWOS)

If the tantrum continues for longer than you can bear and becomes aggressive, or your child becomes non-compliant, or they were aggressive in the first place, use the Time Out technique because these are behaviours that need to be dealt with in another way as simply ignoring is not enough – particularly if someone else has been hurt or is likely to be if the behaviour continues.

I absolutely do not believe that children should be smacked – apart from anything else, why hit them if we don't want them to hit others? So, I recommend the Time Out method – similar to being sent to your room, as I was when I was a child. Time Out is an extreme form of ignoring that allows you to calm down and therefore not react in an impulsive or aggressive manner. It is brief and specific and a very clear message to your child.

Time Out is a last resort approach and must not be used often or instead of more creative and imaginative ways of calming your child's impending rage. If you use this technique too frequently, you have entered a very negative and combative space with your child and need to reassess your attitude towards them.

THE TIME OUT GUIDE

If your child is having a prolonged tantrum or is being non-compliant, you can give them two chances to change their behaviour (once nicely and then once firmly) before Time Out occurs – this enables learning to occur.

So, if you are giving your child a chance to change or stop their behaviour, think carefully about how you ask them to stop: as mentioned earlier, never ask your child or tell your child something more than twice. Think about your tone of voice; think about your non-verbal communications, like your facial expression and eye contact. Get down on their level, look them in the eye and say, 'I want you to stop this now. If you don't stop this, you will go to your room,' and then you walk away. If the behaviour continues, say it again but this time much more firmly: 'I said stop it now. Stop it now, or you will go to your room.'

Aggression, biting, hitting, kicking, hair pulling are all an instant Time Out. It's useful to think of your child's behaviour on a severity scale and you want to help your child learn as quickly as possible that there are some behaviours that are completely unacceptable, particularly as your child starts to go to nursery, where they will be socializing with other children. It's about understanding that behaviour → consequence. And being very clear, and making sure that other people involved in the parenting of your child, the nurturing of your child, are behaving in the same way.

So, with a single incident of aggression (a severe behaviour that cannot be given a 'second chance' to change because it's happened and is entirely wrong), you don't ask twice: it's an immediate Time Out. Make a clear statement: 'You don't bite.' If your child is aggressive, bites or hits or smacks, you just say, 'Right, you're going to your room.' And then you take them to their room for Time Out.

Time Out is managed in a calm manner even if your child is screaming, biting or hitting you as you put them in their room. Leave them there for one minute for each year of their life – up to a maximum of five minutes. There should be no further eye contact or discussion as you are doing this. There is nothing magic about this time formula – it just makes it easy to remember and also ensures that the Time Out period is specified and that a child isn't left in their room indefinitely.

Now, the bit that parents find quite difficult is when their child wants to leave the room. Simply shut the door and hold it. You could say, 'I'm going to hold the door while you're in the room because you kicked your brother/threw your food when I asked you not to, and that is why you're in your room.' Your child might scream and cry and throw things around, getting very, very angry – you just ignore it. You just ignore it. You may find this extremely hard to do but you must not reinforce the behaviour in any way. If you ignore them trashing their room, eventually, they are less likely to do it.

Also remember that their anger is an expression of how disgruntled they are with you for daring to remove your attention from them and therefore the technique is failsafe, especially as it will be coupled with huge amounts of positive attention when they are being lovely.

And then when the two or three or four or five minutes is up, you open the door, get down on their level and say extremely firmly,

'You were put in your room because you hit your brother/threw your food and I asked you not to do it. If you do that again, you will go back in your room.'

Now, if the child then continues with the behaviour and it's non-compliant behaviour, they again get two chances to remedy this. 'I said stop it. If you don't stop it, you're going back in your room,' and if they carry on: 'This is the last time I'm saying this to you – you either stop it now or you're going into your room,' and they go back in if they continue.

If, however, after the period of Time Out they are immediately aggressive again, then they go straight back in – no chances as aggression is just not tolerated once it has occurred, whereas a non-compliant child can learn to change their behaviour and do as they are told in response to a firm voice.

But, if they are obviously calming down, then give them a hug and say, 'Thank you for calming down. Let's go and have a drink,' and then you carry on with the day as if nothing has happened. Do not bear a grudge, do not say, 'Wait till your father comes home,' or 'Wait till your mother comes home.' So much time will have elapsed by then that your child won't remember what it is you are dealing with.

Some parents modify this and will find their own method of Time Out – as I've said before, it's not a one-size-fits-all approach. You might send your child to the corner of the room or out into the hall. Alternatively you could Time yourself Out and remove yourself from them (so long as you are clear that they are safe) for a short period of time.

Overall, Time Out must be implemented only as a last resort and on rare occasions. It must occur somewhere that is safe, well lit and warm. Time Out is not about punishment, it's just about removing your attention from your child – a bit like turning off a tap.

Managing the car/public tantrum

What do you do in the car if they didn't stop after the second time of asking, because there's no Time Out in the car? Or you are in the supermarket and they have a massive tantrum?

In principle, you really just want to aim to diffuse the tantrum by distraction if possible and otherwise by just ignoring (using your nerves of steel). Ignoring is very powerful and really does work but it needs to be done consistently and emotionlessly, which is difficult if you are trapped in a car with a screaming child or in the supermarket with the added burden of the watching public.

Yes, these situations can be a nightmare but you have to ask yourself who is the adult? And, as an adult, OK it's a nightmare because there's a lot of screaming and shouting in the car or, even harder, many eyes looking at you and your child in the supermarket but, as an adult, you can talk yourself down until you get home, and then when you're home and they're still screaming and shouting, you say, 'Right, you can stop that now or you go to your room.' If they carry on, they go to their room or have their favourite toy removed. If they stop, say thank you. However, if you give them what they want to quieten them down, you may have a short-term solution but you are creating a major long-term problem as you teach the child the best way to get what they want from you.

Besides, anyone looking at you in the supermarket, who has kids, has probably been in the same situation. If they look at you in a superior way as if they haven't, they're either lying or have incredibly dull children, who are devoid of personality and spirit!

In situations like this you're doing something called **behaviour shaping**. You're giving your child an understanding of their own behaviour management, so that eventually you can set up a situation where, let's say, you're in the car and the kids are messing around and you say (once nicely), 'Guys, can you stop messing around, please?' and then (once firmly), 'Guys, I mean it, stop messing around,' and the children by this stage have learned that when that face is on, and that tone of voice is on, they should stop.

Naughty stair?

There are other techniques you can use and it's important to develop what works for your family. From a professional and personal view, I'm not a fan of naughty steps, chairs, stairs or naughty mats, because I don't think it is helpful to use anything where it requires you to be physical with your child in order to hold them down in one place and where there is a possibility of it becoming a physical struggle – unless that is necessary for their safety. Time Out removes that possibility in the same way as it stops smacking occurring by allowing you to calm down and gather yourself if necessary in those few minutes of separation.

Holding your child?

However, sometimes with very small children – and I've worked with children who head bang, for example, so putting them in their room is not an option – some parents will hold them on a bean bag, or just hold their child into their body.

If you want to hold your child because you feel it's safer to do that than to leave them in a room where they can hurt themselves, then sit on the floor with your legs open, and hold your child to your body, making sure that you have their head on your chest so they can't head bang you. Hold them secure in a big hug, look away and let them know, calmly: 'When you calm down, this will stop,' and then say nothing further.

You are the best person to know what kind of tantrum your child is having. Some children will feel very out of control when they are having a tantrum and if you hold them firmly they will feel quite contained and will often calm down quite quickly.

When and how often should these techniques be used?

Techniques like taking your child to their room or holding them until they calm down should only be used in extreme situations. You want to avoid that point wherever possible, so concentrate on the other techniques – be creative and develop techniques for distracting your child on the spot, ladle praise on your child more than you admonish them, be prepared to grit your teeth and ignore them. If your child is doing something you don't like, say it once nicely – 'unless you stop you cannot play with that for the rest of the day' – and say it again once firmly. If they still don't stop, take it away and put it on a high shelf where they can see it, so they then have an understanding of the consequences of behaviour.

I want to say again – because it is really important – Time Out and holding your child is the last resort, and it should not be used often. If you are, then you need to think about the fact that you are not getting to the behaviour quickly enough, your child is probably still not getting clear enough messages, or perhaps you're not being quite as creative in your management of the behaviour as possible. It's important to address all these areas before using a last-resort technique.

What if my child's behaviour is related also to emotional issues?

I have worked with families where the behaviour difficulties in the child reflect a number of difficult emotional issues within their relationship with you and possibly the wider family. We will look at this in a more detailed way in Part Three but just for now let's use the example of children whose mother has had or still has post-natal depression/illness (PND/I). Such children are very likely to manifest via their behaviour how they are picking up on the sadness in their mother/family. They may be 'acting up' because they are trying to illicit an emotion, *any emotion*, from a parent who is at that time unable to be emotional and is cut off and removed by their depression.

The parent is not a bad parent – they are an ill parent. The child is not a bad child – they are a worried child.

In such cases a tantrum or uncontrollable rage may be less well managed by a consequence that feels punitive than one that feels understanding. I have worked with parents who have taken their angry child in their arms, held them close and rocked them or, if the tantrum is too severe, just sat on the floor quietly near the child and placed a gentle hand on them or not touched them at all but just been there, their body language saying, 'I'm here for you and can wait until you've finished.'

Now, for those of you that are now totally confused and wondering, 'Do I hug a tantrum away or ignore it or put my child in the corner or in their room or maybe hold them and look away?', my answer is – they are your child, you know them better than anyone and I certainly can't advise you without having met your family. The best way to answer this question is to really analyse your behaviour – is your child needing clear behavioural messages amongst a huge amount of love and praise to be clearer about their behaviour? Or is your child actually showing huge distress and their behaviour reflects something deeper, so they need an approach that is also nurturing? For those of you who are very emotionally responsive to your child already, you need to be careful that cuddling their tantrum away might reinforce it, whereas there may be those of you who need to use that approach because you have not been so emotionally responsive to your child, and they are using their behaviour to communicate that.

Preventive techniques

I've started with the 'reactive techniques' (the 'what to do when it all goes off' techniques), because that is what you were really desperate for. However, I want you to also think about prevention – i.e., ways in which you can stop big behavioural outbursts, effect positive behaviour shaping and so avoid having to do what we've discussed earlier. Ponder this: would you rather put your energy into being fun, spontaneous and creative with your child or constantly having to mete out yet another consequence? Both approaches – the reactive and the preventative – are tiring but being preventive is more fun and bonding: everyone goes to bed with a smile on their face.

STICKER CHARTS

These are both a preventive and reactive technique but given that they are primarily about shoring up the good behaviour as it happens, I'll describe them in this section.

We have already thought about sticker charts in the early days when we were still trying to get our heads into being positive. The chart we did earlier was more for you to train yourself to be positive towards your child and so it didn't really matter the age of the child, but for these that we are now using for the positive behaviour shaping of your child a girl should be three years and boys three-and-a-half years as younger than this each gender cannot really grasp the concept. (The reason for the female/male differentiation is due to the language-age gender difference in young children, which influences understanding.) **Pick a time of day when life is generally fraught** and everyone's behaviour is wearing thin – let's say teatime to bath time: from 5.00 to 6.00 p.m.

Divide a large piece of paper into eight columns and thirteen rows. For the heading of column one write 'Time' and for columns two to eight write the days of the week. For the headings of rows two to twelve the time from 5.00 to 6.00 p.m. in five-minute increments, starting with '5.05' in row two. Start time 5.00. Here's an example:

	Monday	Tuesday	Wednesday	Thursday	Friday	Saturday	Sunday
5.05							
5.10							
5.15							
5.20							
5.25							
5.30							
5.35							
5.40							
5.45							
5.50							
5.55							
6.00							

Let your child design the chart with you so it feels like theirs and that this activity is being done *with* them, not *to* them. They can decorate it, put handprints on it – whatever their creative little hearts desire.

Then set the whole scheme up as excellent fun for all and explain very simply, clearly and calmly that for every five minutes they behave in a lovely way, they will be allowed to go to their chart and put a sticker on it. If they get a lot of stickers, they will get a treat at the end!

When they test out your new boundaries (they will of course be thinking, Who on earth is this parent I see before me?!) they will get asked to behave for their sticker (once nicely and then once firmly). If nothing has changed, they have to watch a sad face being drawn in the time slot. You, of course, will remain neutral and calm and move on positively to the next time slot.

At the end of it all, if your child has at least nine out of twelve slots with stickers in (75%), then they get a treat (there has to be some room for slippage – they are children, after all!).

As the behaviour improves you can use this chart at other times of the day, and increase the time slots until the day is divided into its natural breaks (up to breakfast, up to lunch, up to teatime, up to bedtime). You can even take a mobile version out when shopping (just draw the chart onto a large envelope which can contain pen and stickers – and you're off!).

Be inventive and try other charts. If you want to target specific behaviours recreate a chart like we designed earlier on (for your training!) but this time put in behaviours you really would like to see positive changes in.

A note about rewards: there are soft rewards such as kisses, cuddles, positive attention and hard rewards such as treats. Children love both so don't get yourself into a situation where suddenly for the rest of your life you have to 'buy' your child's good behaviour – go with the soft rewards as much as you can. For charts try little treats in a lucky-dip bag, or pieces of a jigsaw puzzle that can be collected each day, or even an extra ten minutes before bed colouring a special picture. Be creative!

FURTHER CREATIVITY!

So being preventive is about being creative and playing with your child in order to get the best out of them and prevent problem behaviours occurring.

If you know your child hates having their teeth cleaned and you approach it with agitation and the whole event becomes a struggle ending with them in some kind of restraint position on your lap or on the bathroom floor – make it a game. The toothbrush becomes a secret-agent bug zapper and your child's mission (with your help) is to zap all those bugs in their mouth away.

If your child won't put their shoes on – tell them that they probably aren't fast enough to beat you anyway and have a race. (Telling children not to do what you want them to do is often a very effective way of getting them to do it!)

If getting dressed is a struggle – make up a getting-dressed song or game. Close your eyes and say, 'I bet you can't put your vest on by the time I count to ten!'

Have fun, inhabit their world and see these creative, energetic parenting moments as refreshing and the perfect antidote to the stresses of being an adult.

A final note about communication!

If your child doesn't listen to you and you end up yelling a million times 'put your shoes on, put your shoes on, put your shoes on', then your child will become desensitized to your voice and your requests. Likewise, if you use the change of tone in your voice as a signal too often they will become immune to that too. And if you're standing with your back to your children as you're doing the washing up at the sink shouting 'eat your dinner', it's not going to work.

Make your interactions fun and positive – even if you are tired. When you are communicating with your child catch your facial expression in a mirror. Check your body language – are you stiff and tense and so transmitting agitation to your child? Think about how a children's party entertainer engages children with their voice, their expressions and their body language, how they communicate with the children on their level – they can hold a party of twenty three-year-olds enraptured and in the palm of their hand – therefore I'm sure you can do it with one or more of your own children.

OTHER BEHAVIOURS

BREATH HOLDING is rare but some children do it and will have grown out of it by the age of four. There are two types of breath holding: cyanotic (most common) and pallid. The pallid attack is related to fainting usually associated with pain. The cyanotic attack (or blue attack) is seen as largely behavioural whereby the child voluntarily holds their breath as a form of mega protest.

If you are clear that your child's breath holding is cyanotic, then catch it quickly by splashing cold water in their face – the shock will get them breathing again.

If they have started to lose consciousness, do not splash water but leave them as the body will resume breathing again once consciousness is lost (scary but true).

Do not panic or behave in an over-the-top manner when your child starts breathing again as you will reinforce the breath-holding behaviour and they will continue to use it as a lever when they want their own way. Remember it is a form of tantrum so once it is over move on with what you were doing as if nothing has occurred.

If you have any doubt about the breath-holding behaviour or think your child is ill, contact a doctor immediately.

HEAD BANGING can be another tantrum-related behavioural strategy.

Having a pain-regulating mechanism, most children will not bang themselves into unconsciousness although they may sport some bruises on their forehead for a time.

As head banging looks and seems like an aggressive action for a child to do to themselves, understandably parents will panic, rush at their child and make a huge fuss – thus reinforcing the behaviour.

You can ignore it and it will stop eventually as your child learns that there is nothing to gain from it.

Or you can use the gentle but firm holding technique that I described earlier. Hold your child and keep their head on your chest until they calm down. Just look away and try to make your body as relaxed as possible while protecting them, and tell them that when they calm down the holding will stop – then say nothing further.

However, it is important to recognize that some children head bang as a self-soothing mechanism. Some children head bang themselves to sleep, and that's something that you have to think about in a different way. For your child, it's like rocking, sucking a thumb or twiddling a piece of hair. And with parents who have a child who head bangs themselves to sleep, or head bangs when they are self-soothing, you just need to make sure that the environment is safe so they don't hurt themselves. Most children will grow out of it. For boys there is a genetic link: fathers who used head banging as a self-soothing mechanism as a child often have sons that do.

Other factors affecting behaviour

It is important that you also consider whether your child's behaviour is a product of other factors such as what they eat; how much exercise they have and how much they sleep. There isn't room in this book to look specifically at the impact of diet on behaviour and it is probably far too obvious to say that you should be aiming to provide your child with a healthy balanced diet where the foods are mostly cooked from fresh. But do remember that hungry children are more likely to misbehave! Furthermore, many a temper tantrum can be avoided if a child has been given the opportunity to run, jump, climb and get their little hearts and lungs racing. And, indeed – as we all know – a lack of sleep can make the most angelic of us an utter devil.

And this is precisely where we shall turn to next – sleep.

SHE'S PUT A BANANA IN THE VIDEO PLAYER

SLEEP

Sleep is an important part of your child's development and if they do not get enough they are most likely to develop problems with their behaviour, attention and concentration. Does your child get adequate amounts of sleep for their age?

If your child has a sleep problem and you have managed to get this far into the book without sliding into a coma induced by exhaustion – I congratulate you. Lack of sleep is hell, it's torture and indeed not allowing sleep has been used as a form of torture. It's one thing having limited sleep in the early days, weeks and months of getting to know your new baby and creating that bond but, in truth, if your child isn't in a regular sleep pattern past six months (and by this age they should be), you are ready to jump out of a top-floor window.

So, while you are still awake and I have your attention, let me quickly impress on you a few facts that might be helpful to know. Sleep goes in cycles between deep sleep, dreaming sleep, lighter sleep and then we all (adults and children alike) will have brief periods of waking. As adults, when we wake (usually every hour and a half or so) we are not aware of this and will move, adjust our pillows perhaps but then fall straight back to sleep. This is the same for children whose cycle is more likely to be hourly, i.e., they will wake and go back to sleep but may in those periods of waking look around, fiddle with their toys or their comforter or make noises but then drop off again. However, it is essential that children learn the skills of being able to settle themselves off to sleep in the environment that they will wake in through the night – i.e., a dark or dimly lit room in a cot or bed with their familiar comforter or teddy by them. These then become their sleep cues so that when they wake in the night they are cued straight back to sleep – and do this themselves. But if *you* are their cue (your breast, the bottle, your arms rocking them) or there are other environmental cues, such as the television, that they fall asleep to, then these will need to be with them every time they wake as these are what they need to get back to sleep. It's not rocket science but it's easy to fall into the trap of teaching your child the wrong falling-asleep cues and as one parent once said to me – it's a 'living hell' trying to break the child out of them.

Sleep is vital to healthy development and functioning, and it is important to think about the fact that some children have behaviour problems because maybe, primarily, they have a sleep problem. I have worked with many families where a parent will say 'my child behaves badly' but then once we've analysed the daily routine, we find that the child who should be getting eleven hours of sleep is only getting nine hours, so they're actually behaving badly because they're exhausted (in the same way that I bet you're probably a bit snappy and grumpy after a few nights of broken sleep). In that case, sleep is the primary problem and their behaviour secondary, so we have to deal with sleep first.

Below is a table to enable you to look at how much sleep your child should be getting. All children in the toddler age range should be in bed at the latest by 7.30 p.m. and will wake at about 6.30 to 7.00 a.m. But as you calculate the amount of sleep your child has each day remember to add in nap times.

Age	Total sleep (hours)	Night sleep (hours)	No. of naps
6 months	14	11	2
9 months	14	11.5	2
12 months	13	11.5	2
18 months	13	11	1
2 years	12	11	1
3 years	11	11	1
4 years	10-11		
5 years	10.5		

What's the problem?

In my experience there are four main types of sleep problem, and the first thing we need to do is work out what your child's is. Hopefully you can see it now; if you're unlucky, you'll see more than one.

1

The have no bedtime routine: your child may be up all evening and into the early hours, unable to calm down and making demands.

2

They can't fall asleep in their bed: your child falls asleep anywhere but in their own bed – on the sofa, in your arms or even in your bed. You then carry them to their bed and creep out of the room in fear that you will wake them.

3

They won't stay in their bed: your child may not stay in their bed once they've been put in it and will then disrupt your evening by coming downstairs or calling you upstairs with various requests. Or they end up in your bed in the small hours, wriggling and keeping you awake.

4

They wake in the night: your child may call out and cry constantly in the night, wanting drinks, cuddles or attention. You go in, and out, hour after hour, and you're exhausted.

Using a diary

As well as the behaviour diary you found at the back of this book there is a sleep diary that looks like this:

Morning waking time	Times of naps (if appropriate)	Time to bed	How you got your child to sleep	Time to sleep	Time(s) woke in the night	How you got your child back to sleep	Time back to sleep

It is clearly self-explanatory and you really should keep a record for one week before we start to change the situation. Then as you analyse it look at the behaviours around going to cot/bed and your responses – how are you reinforcing the poor sleeping behaviour?

Also, on a piece of paper draw a clock face and shade out the nap and sleep times in a different colour – is your child getting enough sleep? When is your child getting the majority of their sleep? Does their sleep pattern seem to be pushed into the day so night times have become awake times?

Finally, use your diary to decide whether your child has a calm, well-established sleep routine leading up to bedtime that you are in charge of. Look at whether your child can settle themselves and fall asleep alone in their bed/cot from awake in a dark or dimly lit room with no sounds or drinks to suck at (they should be able to do this by six months old). Your diary will obviously tell you the brutal truth that you already know – how long your child can sleep before waking and needing you in the night by either calling out or coming to you. Note the average amount of time you are awake and trying to settle your child and really notice all you are doing to reinforce the wakeful behaviour (by giving drinks, cuddles, chatting, putting the lights on, going downstairs …and so on). Look at how often you get to sleep in your own bed alone or with a partner, but not with a child, and whether that is working for your relationship or not.

Establishing a great bedtime routine

At the heart of many sleep problems I will usually find a poor routine. Unless your child has specific neurological problems, there is no reason why they shouldn't be able to sleep. A good sleep pattern is something that you help your children learn.

Some parents have children who fall into a good sleep pattern easily and some don't but, fundamentally, as parents it is our responsibility to train our children to sleep. From six months onwards they should be in a pattern where you can put them down, they can fall asleep on their own from being awake on their own in a dark or dimly lit room and sleep right through until the morning when they wake and they ask to see you. Within the sleep pattern we all go through various stages of sleep. As adults we often forget waking up. Children will wake through the night on occasion too, and they can and should be able to get themselves back to sleep.

The key thing about sleep is the environmental cues that you set up for your child to sleep. Think about what your child would perceive as being the cue for sleeping. If for your child it's lying on your lap on the sofa sucking on a bottle, while the telly's on, if those are the environmental cues that they have to help them to go to sleep, then they will continue to need those cues because you have conditioned their sleep behaviour around them.

A calm bedtime routine is crucial for children, something similar to this:

Last meal of the day, around 5.30 p.m.
Play for a bit, maybe watch a bit of TV until 6, 6.30 p.m.
Go upstairs, have a warm bath, because if you increase the core body temperature, it can induce sleep, then straight into their pyjamas
Have a final drink
Clean their teeth
Get into bed
Have a story and a song and a kiss and a goodnight
Settle themselves off to zzzzzzzzzz with no props or person nearby

Be aware of your children's arousal levels before they go to bed. Often parents will come home from work, want to play with them and be throwing them in the air and spinning them round, and, of course, the kids are on the ceiling and can't sleep. Also be aware of what your child eats before they go to sleep. If they're drinking lots of fizzy drinks and eating loads of sweets, then that will have an impact on their wakefulness. I think it's important that once little ones are in their pyjamas, they then go straight into bed, still warm and cosy from the bath, and we sit and read to them as a sleep cue. Once you've done that and said goodnight, don't keep popping back in as you will reinforce wakeful behaviour rather than sleep.

The notion of sleep cues is really important. Your child learns that these are the necessary things that help them get off to sleep. Therefore, if you give your child drinks to suck, the TV to watch, your arms to be rocked in or your hands to massage their back into sleep, you will then forever be tied to producing these cues whenever your child wakes in the night.

However, on some of your child's sleeping cues you don't have to go cold turkey, so, for instance, if your child is afraid of the dark and you have been leaving their overhead light on (which is harmful to the quality of sleep), invest in a night light. If you think your child can't go to bed without milk, reduce the amount you give them each night or dilute it with water over time until they lose interest in drinking it.

Make the bedtime routine happy and calm so that your child is cosily steered towards sleep and drops off feeling loved, safe and dreaming happily.

Settling

If you are trying to get your child to settle in bed, there are four key ways to do this: controlled crying, checking, rapid return or gradual withdrawal.

CONTROLLED CRYING

With controlled crying, follow the bedtime routine outlined above, say goodnight and leave.

If they scream and cry, but they're still in their bed, you can either leave them for a while or go in, pat them and just say, 'Shhhh, it's bedtime/night time – it's time to go to sleep,' and walk out, but be very low key so that your response is non-reinforcing. You can do this for increasing lengths of time, so at first you can leave them for five minutes before going back in to reassure them again that you are there, before leaving straight away. But be very non-reinforcing each time you go to them. Be really boring. Don't make eye contact; keep your voice very low, very dull. Just go in, say, 'Shhh, shhh, shhh,' and go out.

And then just leave it for increasing amounts of time up to a maximum of fifteen minutes.

This is about not reinforcing the behaviour you don't want because as soon as you pick them up and give them a cuddle they'll do it again, because cuddles are great! So it's about just being firm, which I know emotionally is difficult as a parent, but after a few nights of this it'll all be forgotten and over, and your child will be sleeping through till morning.

I strongly believe that you shouldn't leave your child crying for longer than a fifteen-minute spell because after that time they have actually been crying for half an hour in total: 5 + 10 + 15 = 30 minutes. By this stage abandon the approach because I am sure that not only is your child so distressed and becoming stressed, you are also distressed and are highly unlikely to be able to give them a calm and reassuring message each time you go in.

Also, apart from becoming exceedingly stressed, there is a chance that having had a last drink before bed, your child is likely to vomit it up. If they do, just go in and, with as little fuss as possible, without big cuddles or anything, you just take off their clothes, wipe them, put new ones on and lie them down. Then try another technique – checking.

CHECKING
Use this approach if you don't feel comfortable with the controlled crying method or you have found it too distressing for you and your child.

Check your child at five-minute intervals. Keep the intervals at five minutes and do not increase the time.

At these five-minute intervals go in calmly even if your child is crying and say, 'Shhh, it's bedtime/night time – it's time to go to sleep.' Then you can leave your child for five minutes safe in the knowledge that you don't have to go in for another five minutes but that doesn't feel too long a time for you or your child. This means that you are more likely to then be able to give a clear, confident and containing message.

This method usually works within three to five nights.

RAPID RETURN
The third technique is rapid return, when your child won't stay in bed.

You simply wait outside the door, and literally just walk them back to their bed every time they get up. You put them back in bed and walk out. You have to be prepared before you embark on this technique, as it can be emotionally and physically exhausting in the short term. I have had an extreme example of a couple who had to return their child approximately 300 times in one night. But the good news was then that was it. The child slept from the next night on in their own bed.

If your child is having a tantrum at the same time as getting out of bed, you have to lift them onto the bed, put them down, cover them and walk out, but be non-reinforcing, don't talk to them, don't make a big fuss, but very consistently, very boringly, take them back and walk out, take them back and walk out. Even if your child bites or kicks you – ignore this and just place them in the bed, cover them and walk out.

If after your child has been asleep for a while, they then wake in the night and come to your bed, repeat this procedure – do it in shifts with a partner if you can. If you don't hear your child coming into your room and then wake in the night/morning to find them there, put bells on your door or sew them round the bed so that you can hear your little night companion coming in!

Many parents start sleep training and then stop it because they become desperate that it's not working and they are so exhausted. You need to be fully prepared in using this behavioural approach that the behaviour will often get worse before it gets better. As you set a new boundary your child will fight against it because they're used to being able to control you with their behaviour rather than you being the one in charge.

Keep a small notebook outside the room when you start sleep training and keep a record of how many times you return your child. Perhaps on the first night you might have to return them sixty times, the second night seventy-five times, the third night forty times and the fourth night twenty times. Think of it like plotting a graph. If you can see the overall progress, and you can accept that it will get worse before it gets better, you will keep going. Don't give up on the second night.

And, if you're parenting with a partner or if you're a single parent and you have a friend who can help you, see this as a real project that you're going to crack, and when you've done fifteen, twenty, thirty returns and you're exhausted, swap over. Your child will then see that everybody's doing the same thing so it's a good, consistent message.

GRADUAL WITHDRAWAL

If you feel your child's sleep problem is anxiety related, or if you feel too anxious yourself to be able to rapid return, then try the gradual withdrawal technique.

When you put your child to bed, sit on the floor near them, or maybe if your child is very used to you lying with them to go to sleep, lie there and have a bit of your body touching them but look away and say nothing. If your child tries to engage you, simply say, 'Shhh, shhh, shhh.'

If your child gets up, lie them down, look away and say nothing, and over the next few nights gradually withdraw the physical proximity to your child. So you might sit on the end of the bed, then you might sit on the floor in the middle of the room, then you might sit on a chair by the door, then you might sit outside the door.

Your child is literally becoming disentangled from you. This is very useful if you have a child who is used to falling asleep on a parent, or near a parent, or being rocked or held. Rapid return can induce extreme anxiety for those children because it's a massive separation. However, some children can become so demanding and get so cross when parents do gradual withdrawal that just the physical act of being there in the room is too reinforcing. If this is the case, you may have to be brave and go for rapid return and although you might have a very cross child for a short period of time, if you follow the technique consistently over time, you and your child will be fine.

QUESTION – WHAT ABOUT THE DOOR-SHUTTING TECHNIQUE?

The door-shutting technique is where you hold the door shut and you say to your child, 'When you get into your bed I'll open the door.' I think at night, in darkness or semi-darkness, this technique can induce more fear in a child, so I don't recommend it. I don't like the notion of the door being shut at night times.

USING A STICKER CHART

Again, for girls over the age of three, boys over three and a half, sticker charts can be very powerful at shaping behaviour. Here is an example:

Day	Stay in bed	Go straight to sleep
Monday	✗	✗
Tuesday	✔	✔
Wednesday	✔	✗
Thursday	✔	✔
Friday	✔	✗
Saturday	✔	✔
Sunday	✔	✔

Use magic and creativity to induce a sense of excitement and wonderment around the chart – maybe it belongs to the night-time fairy and she will leave little stars for children who sleep well in the morning. Make it achievable for your child and so start with what they can do (i.e., get nicely into pyjamas) and then build slowly, making the rewards harder to earn.

Waking in the night

As we discussed at the beginning of this section, your child will wake briefly throughout the night as they move through the different sleep cycles (approximately every sixty minutes or so). As we also thought about, if your child has learned to fall asleep in their room alone (and from six months there is no reason why they can't), then when they wake in the same room that signals sleep to them they will be able to drift off again by themselves. However, if you have given them other sleep cues that are not present when they wake in the night, such as something associated with you or something else like the television or a bottle to suck on, your child will require those cues to be brought to them (by you) in order for them to get back to sleep.

This is the killer of it all because, in the night when you are probably asleep and then abruptly woken (especially because your and their wake cycles will rarely coincide – yours at ninety minutes, theirs at sixty minutes), what you now have to do is twofold:

1 Help them unlearn their dependence on the inappropriate night-time cues;
2 Help them learn appropriate sleep associations that don't require you to be there.

You can do this by firstly establishing a routine for going to bed and falling asleep as we have discussed above – a routine that is calm and reflects the task in hand – falling asleep. A routine that ends with you leaving your child and using a controlled-crying, checking, rapid-return or gradual-withdrawal technique to establish the new sleep cues. For most children over the age of two and a half the learning at bedtime will transfer seamlessly into the night-waking behaviour as the bedtime learning occurs. However, in the phase of learning you need to adopt the same strategy in the night as you did at bedtime and this might be tough. But, if you keep telling yourself that your child is learning, you will be able to bear the few nights (two weeks maximum if you are consistent in your approach). Some tips to help you through:

In order to help you succeed with the sleep training and not to fall apart with exhaustion in the process, I suggest that you tackle teaching your child to go to sleep at bedtime (when their tiredness is on your side) first. In other words, maximize success by separating the bedtime and night-time training phases.

A colleague of mine once did a small study and found that 90% of over two-and-a-half-year-olds, once they had learned to fall asleep properly in their bed alone at bedtime, transferred that learning across to the night. So, if they woke in the night, they would then just settle themselves back to sleep without needing any training. This is related to language development mediating learning.

For the remaining 10% that don't transfer their learning from bedtime to night time, or are under two and a half, it will take only one week of night training for them to learn if you consistently use the exact same strategy as you did when training them at bedtime.

So, during the first (bedtime) stage of training your child, you can happily continue to do the 'wrong' thing at night, knowing that your child is either:

too young to work out that you are dealing with them differently at bedtime and then in the night and so will respond to the bedtime training if it happens consistently each bedtime; or

old enough to question the difference in your approach but then also old enough to be told that that's just the way that things are being done.

If you have a partner, do the training in shifts. If you don't, ask a friend or relative to help either in the night or by having your child in the daytime so you can get some sleep.

Again, if your child is a creature of stealth and gets into your bed without your knowledge, then put bells on your door or stitch them round your bed – anything so you can wake and quickly, calmly and efficiently get them back to bed with little reinforcement.

If your child wakes for a drink, it is probably because they want to suck themselves to sleep. Very wet nappies in the morning indicate a child who is well hydrated and doesn't need the fluid in the night. You can either stop them immediately, reduce the amount of milk in the beaker each night or water the drink down by increasing amounts each night.

Other night-time problems

NIGHT TERRORS, NIGHTMARES AND SLEEPWALKING

Some children will wake in the night, and while they look awake and agitated and may scream out they will not be aware of you being there. These night terrors occur during deep-sleep stages and will not be remembered by the child in the morning, but will be very distressing for you. There are two approaches to use:

Record the timings of the night terrors. If you find that they are occurring in the same hour every night, then they are related to sleep-wave pattern. In this case you can wake your child half an hour before the time you know the night terrors will occur and so, by disrupting their sleep-wave pattern at that time, avoid the terror happening. After a few nights of this the terror should stop.

However, if the night terror does not occur in a regular time slot, then the thinking is not to wake your child, and to just be around them to make sure that they're safe and don't hurt themselves. If you get very anxious and wake your child, this might upset them and end up making the problem worse. You should find that your child will eventually lie themselves down and go back to sleep, and will grow out of it, with no treatment required.

Like self-soothing head banging, which children may also do to settle themselves to sleep (see page 85), night terrors are often seen in sons of fathers who also experienced them.

It's a similar situation with nightmares and sleepwalking. Nightmares usually occur in the rapid-eye-movement stage of sleep (the light stage) and require a comforting presence to calm the child and sit quietly with them until they fall back to sleep without fear.

Sleepwalking occurs during deep-sleep stages and is never remembered: again more common in males and running in the family. Clearly, if you have a child who sleepwalks, make sure you keep their environment as safe as possible.

BEDWETTING

If your child has a problem with bedwetting then see page 132 in toilet training.

FEAR OF THE DARK

If your child has a fear or anxiety of bed, or of the dark, again you can use the gradual withdrawal technique, but this time you could be more creative. You could, for example, put a small squeeze bottle by the bed, and make up a story that it's a special monster zapper. Or create a special little game to make the room feel safe, or put magic stars on the ceiling. Work on the level of a child's world, rather than your world. Think about the stories they respond to and what element of a favourite story could help you resolve the problem.

Some children respond well to a comforter, with maybe just a squirt of your perfume on it. Or, with very small ones whom you're sleep training, you could put muslin in your clothes during the day, and then leave it tied to the bars of the cot, or in the bed, so the child has your smell close by. So think laterally about how to solve the problems.

Some children will ask to sleep with the overhead light on – a night light just won't do. However, bright light during sleep can affect the sleep-wave pattern and lead to poor sleep quality. Some families I have worked with have installed a dimmer switch on their child's bedroom light and gradually reduced the illumination over time.

SIBLINGS

You might be worried that your child will wake the sibling they share a room with while you are trying to make changes to their sleep behaviour. Often this doesn't happen if the sibling is already in a deep sleep. Sometimes the sibling may be awake but stays in bed and eventually falls asleep even with the commotion going on. On occasion a very noisy and protesting child might wake their sibling and, if this happens, take the sibling out of the room and put them into your bed to sleep while you persevere with the sleep programme. If the sibling is already a good sleeper, then it won't be too disruptive.

EARLY WAKING

If your child is an early riser, you can use a sticker chart as a means of rewarding them symbolically for not coming to you straight away and playing quietly in their room. You can also get clocks, which show a child via a moving animal face when it is a reasonable hour for them to wake others. Also, you could attach a simple digital timer to a lamp and tell them that it is OK to be awake and come into your room when the light comes on – start with the earliest point that your child wakes and then set the light to come on slightly later each day.

If your child is still having naps, consider whether they are sleeping too much in the day. Also, if from your diary you calculate that your child is already getting the required amount of sleep, it might be sensible to put them to bed slightly later with the aim to push the sleep into a later waking in the morning. Frustratingly, most young children don't understand the notion of a weekend lie in and there's nothing you can do about that!

MAKING BEDTIME EARLIER

If you are intending to use one of the approaches we have described and your child goes to bed very late, do not set yourself up to fail by initially putting your child to bed too much earlier. It's best to start at a time near to the bedtime the children are used to and then cut it back by ten minutes each night until they get to a good bedtime. You can work out what this bedtime would be by using the sleep requirements chart and working backwards from when your child usually wakes up.

DON'T SET YOURSELF UP TO FAIL

If you are tackling a number of problems, give yourself a chance to succeed by taking them one at a time. Establish a good bedtime routine before you tackle the night waking. Each bit of learning will help towards resolving the other problem behaviour. What I suggest is that you keep a record of the number of returns each night or the number of wakings so that you can see progress. If your child wakes twenty-three times one night and eighteen times the next – that is progress although, if you haven't recorded it, you may not feel that there is any progress and will give up. Remember that learning takes time and also that when helping children learn any new behaviour you will often find, as I've said before, that their behaviour will initially get worse before it gets better. Hold on to that thought and don't give up!

PHENERGAN/VALLERGAN
(PROMETHAZINE HYDROCHLORIDE)

These are both sedating antihistamines: Phenergan can be bought over the counter; Vallergan needs to be prescribed (not for under-twos) and is normally used as an anti inflammatory in the management of eczema in children. They may cause drowsiness and so are sometimes used with children who don't sleep well. I think that parents should resort to these medicinal measures only on the advice of their GP and when the situation is really desperate. By 'desperate' I mean that you, the parent, who has to do the sleep training, simply does not have enough sleep credit in your own bank, and so to do any kind of behaviour training would not be physically possible for you. After you've got some sleep, while your child sleeps given the sedating effects of Phenergan/Vallergan, you would then wean them off as you implement the sleep training. In essence, the medications act as scaffolding until you feel able to erect the building and take the scaffolding down.

However, if you are not in absolute dire straits, have some energy and would rather not use medication with your child, your knowledge that sleep is a learned behaviour will get you through a sleep-training programme.

A final thought

It is really important to say that the sleep training outlined in this section is for use by those of you who genuinely feel there is a problem with your child's sleep behaviour. A problem would mean that they are not getting enough sleep to ensure strong and positive development, that a lack of sleep is seen via daytime behaviour problems, which make everyone feel miserable, or that maybe your relationship with your partner feels compromised by a lack of sleep and alone time in bed together. If any of these issues exist for you and your family, then obviously you will have taken the steps we have discussed. However, I do not want to give the impression that I believe the decision made by a family to have their child sleep in the parental bed is inappropriate. Not at all – and, in fact, in some cultures children do sleep with their parents until the child feels ready to move into their own bed or they reach school age – and that works well for them.

There is also the debate about the physiological effects of leaving children crying for long periods and how harmful that could be to them. I think this all has to be thought about in the larger context of how the family functions as a whole. I certainly don't subscribe to leaving a child to cry for long periods of time. However, if your child has cried over a few nights of training with you being a periodic reassuring but non-reinforcing presence and now they sleep soundly, you sleep soundly and the home feels happier and more harmonious, then that is an outcome that must be balanced against the action taken to bring it about.

Also, you may be wondering about schools of thought that recommend very precise sleep/nap/feed training for children from birth. I do know families who have done this and feel positive about it and also others who have tried it and felt like they'd failed if they weren't doing it 'properly'. My view is that you should find what works best for you. As a mother and a child psychologist I would say that *I* am not comfortable with the notion of precise routines from the outset, as I do think the early weeks and months are to do with the creation of a bond – thus the child should not be viewed as a task but as a new precious and bewildered little human being.

You and your child need to get to know each other in these very early days and that means you should feel able to lift them when they cry in the night and let them fall asleep on your breast if that feels right for you and them. You may feel like you're reinforcing all the wrong behaviours and, yes, life may feel disorganized but isn't that what it's like to fall in love? Build the bond, establish a relationship and a trust, so that as you move into healthy sleep patterns your little one knows your sounds and smells and won't feel abandoned: the bond is there.

Your child will flourish and develop with good sleep routines and patterns. Furthermore, your family will enjoy being a family if everyone is sleeping well. How and where you choose the sleep to be is your choice and one that must be made with the best interests of everyone at heart.

EATING

Can we as parents feel any more anxious about our children than when we think about feeding them? I can remember holding my new baby daughter in my arms and suddenly feeling completely overwhelmed by the responsibility of keeping her alive and healthy. Our first foray together into feeding via my breast was both the most magical and the most committed experience I'd ever had and then a few months later I'd find myself mashing up vegetables for her to try – I never mash vegetables if I can possibly help it.

Clearly, we should all be conscientious to make sure that what goes into our children is as good as it can be – we should treat our children like high-performance cars and ensure that the fuel we put in is premium grade. However, there is plenty of evidence to suggest that we are struggling to feed our children as we are now seeing both alarming rates of childhood obesity and, at the other end of the spectrum, younger and younger children presenting with eating difficulties. Over the seventeen years of my practice as a clinician, I am also seeing a steady increase in the numbers of families who are coming to me with concerns about eating.

So, what is going on? With any child behaviour there will be complex and myriad factors that influence that behaviour. But seeing as we are in the practical stage of our journey, we should stick to considering your role in the problems your child has with their eating, and how, by changing your behaviour, we can positively change theirs. The 'what could be underneath all this?' question comes later in Part Three.

To keep things simple, I would say that your child's eating problems probably lie in one or maybe more of the categories below:

1

They don't eat much and have a very limited diet, leaving you feeling extremely anxious about their healthy development.

2

They are fussy and faddy about what they eat – taking control and leaving you feeling frustrated and helpless.

3

They behave badly at the table or may not even eat at a table, leaving you feeling angry and embarrassed.

4

They show extreme anxiety when touching or being asked to eat certain types and textures of foods – recoiling and getting distressed, leaving you feeling similarly upset.

RECORD THE PROBLEM

As with any behaviour problem, there is no point in starting
any types of 'treatment' before we are completely clear about
the nature of the issue itself. Here is an example of a very simple
food diary (also found at the back of the book) and I urge you
to keep it for at least a week.

Day *Monday*

Time	9.00
Meal, snack or drink	Breakfast
What you gave and how much	Small bowl of porridge and a small glass of orange juce
What the child has eaten and where	4 spoonfuls of porridge and all the orange juice, in the kitchen
Length of meal	15 minutes
What the child did	Refused to sit at table. Didn't want to eat.
What you did	Persuaded her to eat 4 spoonfuls, then gave up

It's simple and self explanatory and the key point is to keep a
detailed record of everything your child eats throughout the day,
the amount and type of food eaten, snacks, drinks and the time
of eating and the place where food is eaten. Specify quantities
as precisely as you can even down to the number of chips,
spoonfuls of yoghurt or the bites of cracker!

As we've discussed before, once you start to monitor your
child's behaviour and your behaviour, things will begin to change.
As you look at your diary think about the following:

- Do I behave in a way that would make anyone want to eat? (Focus on overuse of wipes; thrusting spoons at little mouths; nagging and cajoling endlessly.)
- Is there a good mealtime routine? (Look at the times of eating; the place of eating; whether you can distinguish between snack time and mealtime.)
- Is my child actually hungry at mealtime? (Notice whether you allow them to fill up on snacks and sweet or milky drinks between mealtimes.)
- Does my child get enough exercise for them to require refuelling at mealtimes?
- Who is the adult at mealtimes? (Notice who has the control over what is eaten, where it is eaten and how it is eaten. Do you give your child endless choices about their diet?)
- What is my attitude towards feeding my child? (Are you calm? Is eating fun? Or are you anxious and the whole process of eating fraught and threatening?)

You probably don't need a clinical psychologist to help you answer these questions. Nor do you really need me to spell out what's probably blindingly obvious – your child isn't eating because they probably have too much control at mealtimes and because the whole process may be infused and polluted by your anxious behaviour. So, please try this the next time you have a meal – ask a partner or friend to serve you something you are not particularly fond of, wipe your mouth endlessly with a perfumed wipe throughout the meal and adopt a stressed attitude with you – possibly thrusting spoonfuls of your meal at your mouth. Does that make you want to eat? I doubt it. So then what happens? Well, you probably give up on your meal, wander off and then an hour or so later start to feel really hungry and so you grab a couple of biscuits, maybe some crackers and cheese and a few cups of milky coffee to keep you going. And at the next mealtime – you're not hungry, and again I want you to be met by a stressed and anxious dining partner.

I think you understand my point.

If you want your child to eat in a relaxed fashion and enjoy their food as well as embracing a varied and nutritionally healthy diet, you need to change your approach to their feeding. So, before you do anything else, I want you to try the following:

On a piece of paper, define clear mealtimes and clear snack times. No snack should be given less than an hour before a mealtime. Draw this up as a timetable and write in the foods and drinks to be given at each time.

Snack times should not be times of huge food intake, however hungry and grumpy your child is. A few crisps or pieces of fruit (if your child will eat fruit) plus non-filling drinks. Milk should only be given within each meal, on waking, at bedtime and nap times, but never close to a meal. Water should be given in unlimited amounts throughout the day to ensure hydration – if your child refuses water, give them the weakest diluted fruit juice (you can weaken over time so they get used to the taste).

Your child's stomach is smaller than an adult's (about the size of their fist) – so give them small, manageable portions. Give them very little so they ask for more.

Food should be eaten at a table with no television on (including, at the moment, snacks). If you need to entertain your child, tell them stories, sing songs, make eating a game.

Limit the mealtime to fifteen minutes and without any fuss or pressure just end the meal, whatever has been eaten, and don't feed again until the snack time and then only give a small snack.

What we are aiming to achieve here is a good eating routine where eating times are separate and most feeding is done at the main mealtimes not snack times. Also, your child is not being forced to eat or hovered over anxiously or being over-wiped. Finally, by limiting feeding time, discarding uneaten food without a fuss and not over-snacking you are also allowing your child to begin to recognize physiological cues of hunger, which will compel them to eat better at the next mealtime.

FURTHER ANALYSIS

As is already clear, your behaviour is having the most profound impact on your child's behaviour. What I am really suggesting is to take a step back from your child's actual diet and eating behaviour and let them eat what they like within a well-defined feeding routine, and in an atmosphere free of tension and anxiety. This will make a profound difference to the problems and your ability to solve them over time. However, a few words of caution.

There are some children who have problems eating because there are a number of factors involved including organic (physical) problems. So, it may well be that although there are behaviours from both you and your child that have led to the problem behaviour, they are underpinned by organic difficulties that need further investigation, such as problems with the development of the oral musculature or congenital difficulties of the intestinal tract. It is important, therefore, for you to think carefully about what you believe you are seeing in terms of your child's behaviour and get a comprehensive medical assessment if you have any concerns at all.

From a psychological and emotional point of view, as we have already established, it is not difficult to see why we feel anxious about feeding our child, given the primitive and fundamental role of food in our child's life. However, as discussed in Part One, anxiety is a behaviour in response to feeling threatened and this can lead us to either fight or withdraw. In analysing yourself and your child's behaviour, I suspect you are either both fighting at mealtimes or one of you is the aggressor and the other just withdraws or you both have just given up totally – all behaviours underpinned by anxiety. Please revisit the anxiety management discussion in Part One and then begin to think about how you can feed your child in a calm and positive manner.

DOES MY CHILD HAVE A PROBLEM?

Here's a quick checklist:

Your child should be able to self-feed from about ten to twelve months onwards (or younger if their motor skills can facilitate the process). Your child should not have control over their choice of foods or their diet, because their taste palate, or range of tastes, is not yet fully developed.

From weaning onwards, your child should be able to enjoy a range of fresh foods from across all the food groups.

Toddlers are often neophobic – which means they are instinctively frightened of anything new or unfamiliar. This includes anxiety about new flavours and textures. However, with gentle encouragement over time, their diet will expand.

From the age of four months a child should be able to take food into their mouth, push it to the back of their mouth and swallow it, with biting and chewing beginning at around six months.

A child who has a healthy diet and will sit and eat their food can, however, be given a small number of food choices as an incentive, as they have no issues relating to food.

Your child should be consuming enough calories to be a good weight for their height (get your GP or health visitor to check this for you). Your child should be eating a good range of foods and getting a healthy balance in their diet.

Your responses to the above will tell you how much of a problem you and your child have. You may have already found that by simply making a routine, calming down, keeping a time-limited mealtime, feeding at a table and limiting snacks your child is improving. In that case, well done! However, if you feel there is more to be done – read on!

Further practical steps

I am going to offer a very simple and practical series of techniques that you can tailor to your child's needs.

STEP 1

Chill out. You've already started to bring your anxiety levels down using some of the techniques outlined in Part One. You should be approaching mealtimes by talking to yourself positively and taking yourself away from the negative and anxious thoughts that will set up a pattern of behaviour that will ultimately lead to your child not eating well. You are being calm and firm and are clear about the rules. You are using songs and games to keep the atmosphere positive and get your child to the table.

Look at your anxiety and how it affects your behaviour – don't hover over your child or stare at them intently (you try eating in those conditions)! Children often eat or try a new food when they think they are not being watched so you could have your back to them at the sink and watch them with a strategically placed mirror. If your anxiety is huge, then take a step back and let a less stressed partner or parent or friend begin to imbue mealtimes with fun and a sense of calm while you take a less active role. But still remain present if possible so you are associated with the new calm environment.

STEP 2

Be a positive role model. You should sit and eat with your child. If they don't know how to eat, you will need to model appropriate feeding skills so that they can observe, copy and learn. Be kind and be patient, making it fun without any pressure or expectation for them to actually put anything in their mouth. Make lots of 'yummy' noises. Any copying and possible eating should be rewarded with praise, cuddles and laughter.

3

Have fun. Tell stories about the food; give them characters. Arrange the food into shapes and make faces on the plate. Allow your child to join in with preparation and let there be mess. Play an eating game or set your child up to beat you by picking up the carrot first or licking the sweetcorn. Often telling a child they mustn't eat and closing your eyes with lots of dramatic instructions not to eat will entice them to do it!

4

Positive reinforcement. Link your positive attention to eating, sitting nicely and trying new foods and ignore behaviour that is related to the eating problem. If you've got more than one child at the table, attend to the child that is eating and ignore the one that isn't. Use every communication outlet that you can – both verbal and non-verbal. Remember that your tone of voice, your body posture and your facial expression can put a 'well done' dead if you are showing frustration and stress through them.

STEP 5

Set a routine and boundaries. Who is in charge? Your child, as soon as they are able, should be encouraged to self-feed – however messy this is – and have control over how the food gets into them. However, they should not be in control of their mealtimes, diet or nutritional choices – that is your role as their parent and is the same as you setting the bedtimes and making sure they have regular washes and clean their teeth. You wouldn't leave this for them to take control over would you? (If you do, then you need to read all other parts of this section!) So, be clear about what you want your child to do and when it will happen and within what time frame. You should have already decided this earlier on so, to enforce your routine and boundaries, ask once nicely and then once more firmly with lots of praise for doing as asked and lots of creative energy invested in turning them away from tantrum and refusal. If their behaviour is completely unacceptable, use a firmer consequence – maybe a toy on a high shelf or no yoghurt for pudding. This will be short term while they learn the new rules.

Set realistic goals. Don't run before you walk and don't expect your child to swallow before they can chew. Draw a ladder and at the bottom rung write what your child is currently able to do/eat while at the top rung write what you want them to do/eat. On the rungs in between both those positions write smaller steps to get you from bottom to top:

• If your child will only eat blended food, but should be chewing and swallowing, your small steps would include presenting familiar foods and tastes less and less blended over time, as well as allowing your child to play with other foods and, as a game, lick them, kiss them and eventually get them in their mouth, starting with slow-dissolve foods such as sponge fingers.

• If your child won't try new foods, just present them on the plate but let them be rejected or pushed aside. Research shows that children need at least fifteen to twenty presentations of food before they will even contemplate trying it – each presentation is a small step, a rung up the ladder.

• If your child will only eat from a certain plate with food in a certain shape and with only the purple spoon, just make small and subtle shifts to change this fixed and rigid behaviour over time. Take this at your child's pace.

Make positive food associations. As described above, this is a way of extending the range of foods eaten by a picky eater. Introduce a small amount of the new food alongside the familiar food. In that way the flavour and texture of the new food gradually becomes familiar – and the known food acts as a treat. You must not force the pace. Do a little at a time, some each day. Try not to lead, but give your child lots of encouragement and praise. If your child doesn't want to put the food in their mouth, encourage them to touch it or smell it, so that they become familiar with what it is. This should all feel fun and non-threatening. If the only way to get mashed potato into your child is to let it go in initially with a piece of chocolate button plonked in the middle of it – so be it!

YOUR CHILD . . . YOUR WAY

118

8

Tolerate mess. If your child has a problem with touch and texture of food and is not willing to try new foods, particularly wet or sloppy foods, the chances are they have developed a slight phobia (fear). You can spot this if, for example, your child gets food or paint or soil or anything on their hands, body or clothes that they don't like and they stretch their hands out, wanting to be wiped. You can identify this problem and also overcome it by setting up regular messy play sessions – papier maché is a good one, or maybe making a picture with different foods: cooked pasta, baked beans, squeezy sauces, etc.

However, the reason that you are probably wincing as you read this is because you are a neat, clean parent who will clear up immediately, maybe even disinfecting your home within an inch of its life. Maybe your children's toys are in boxes neatly labelled and maybe you'd prefer if they stayed there rather than be played with and messed up. Maybe it bothers you when your child goes out to play in their lovely washed clothes and new shoes and so you keep them out of the sand pit, away from the muddy path and definitely nowhere near the puddles. If you are this parent, you are now laughing as you read this because you know what I am going on to say. Yes – it's all because of you! You've

role modelled this fear of dirt and mess and, as far as eating goes, this can cause big problems, which you are now seeing. You must role model getting messy and dirty – let your child paint your face with chocolate mousse and blob tomato ketchup on your nose – only you can show them that there is nothing to be afraid of. Make this part of your play routine (in other words you are regularly desensitizing them to their fear) and take lots of photos that you can bring out at their twenty-first birthday party. Also, at mealtimes let them feed themselves with their fingers – even jelly and yoghurt! And LOCK THE WET WIPES AWAY.

PS: If you are the parent outlined above also consider this:

• Children need to experience dirt and bacteria in order to develop strong and healthy immune systems.
• Imaginative, exploratory play develops cognitive skills – don't compromise this by not allowing the toys to be scattered around for a while or forbidding anything that might be a bit risky or involve dirt or mess.

Have a family cold-baked-bean food fight in the garden. OK, maybe that's pushing you too far, but you get my drift – let your child be a child.

Motivate your child. Sticker charts are a wonderful way to motivate your child and also remind you to be a positive, optimistic parent rather than a grumpy, critical one. Here's an example for children who need to learn how to behave:

	Alice	Bella	Charlie
Sit nicely			
Feed yourself			
Eat what you are asked to			
Try/lick/kiss one new food			

It's not complicated and, actually, by involving other children and maybe making this process (behaviour shaping) into a game or competition (invite well-eating friends over to take part) you can use the competitiveness that infuses groups of older children to get them all going. The trying of a new food should be judged against what rung your child is currently on on their ladder – for some it might be eating a Brussels sprout, for others kissing and licking a single piece of sweetcorn. If your child gets all four stickers, they can then choose their reward: a favourite pudding; a game to play with you after supper; ten minutes' more time up before bed to read a comic book with you. If they don't achieve but others do, you have to grit your teeth and let them not get their reward when others do – learning sometimes has to be tough to be effective.

10

Pulling together. As we have discussed in other sections, there is absolutely no point in trying to change your child's behaviour in a positive direction, by interacting with them in a positive, optimistic and nurturing way, if others involved in their care are not interacting with them in the same way. Children need clarity in terms of what is expected of them in the same way that you were hoping for clarity from me and this book in terms of feeling secure and confident. Mixed messages lead to confusion and are probably accompanied by a stressful atmosphere and moments of argument as you and your partner disagree about what should be done. Therefore, you must agree the strategy with all others and look at ways you can support each other when one is finding it tough. Have a code word for when you can see that your partner or others feeding your child is about to lose it and with a strategically uttered 'courgette' let them leave the room and then take over infusing the room with calm, confidence and a lightness of touch in a way that makes Mary Poppins look like Attila the Hun.

11

The tough/nurture balance. Helping your child develop healthy and age-appropriate food behaviours and eating habits as well as a nutritionally balanced diet takes more time to achieve than correcting a sleep problem or dealing with tantrum behaviour. You need to be patient and realize that this process can take a much longer time (weeks/months). Food and eating should be one of life's pleasures and so your approach must reflect this whereas your behaviour in the past has probably signalled stress and anxiety. However, I have worked with families who have taken a very tough stance with their children and stopped all foods that they want to eat and presented them with tiny portions of a new food and have literally sat through a Mexican stand off for more than an hour patiently telling their child to eat the speck of bread, for example, and then ignoring all tantrum and sick behaviour. The child then got nothing to eat until the next meal (but was kept well hydrated) and the whole battle of wills began again. If this is done consistently, with an enormous amount of patience and huge kisses and cuddles when finally the speck is eaten and swallowed, it can transform eating behaviour quickly. But, if you don't like the sound of this approach, use the plan I have outlined in this chapter – taking a clear, routine-based and consistent approach that slowly helps your child to shift their feeding behaviour.

You know your child – you are their parent and hopefully you are beginning to feel like (or are getting to be) a confident and positive parent.

So, whatever you choose to do – it's your call. Just make sure you take it slowly, be calm and make sure everyone has fun.

Obesity

A book that tackles feeding and eating in children cannot ignore the alarming rise in childhood obesity. Obesity in children will have implications for their development and long-term health as well as their social functioning in a society where those who are overweight will often feel ridiculed, teased and even bullied.

Obesity can exist because of excessive calorie intake or possibly a family vulnerability to obesity (in these cases weight gain would be slow and steady through early childhood) or maybe because of a difficult and traumatic emotional experience (weight gain in this case would be sudden and rapid) or (as is usually the case) a combination of the above. If you have concerns that your child is overweight, you should first visit your GP or health visitor who can weigh and measure your child exactly and if necessary refer you to a dietician.

At home, look at your child's feeding behaviour and your role in it. If it seems that there is a problem with saying NO to food requests, then look in the behaviour section for advice on saying no to children and dealing with their tantrums. Make sure you have spaces between feeding times as many overweight children tend to graze throughout the day – so look at your routines around meal and snack times. Try to improve the quality of food eaten by using the techniques described earlier, and at all times maintain a positive outlook, never making your child feel there is something wrong with their eating behaviour.

With obesity as well as restrictive eating it is also very important to consider your own relationship with food and eating – you are your child's role model, so how much of their behaviour do they get from you? Are you constantly on a diet or find you can't control your urge to binge? These issues will be addressed in Part Three and are essential for you to think about if you want to maintain the positive changes that you have made to your child's behaviour.

TOILET TRAINING

Often within family mythology there will be a relative of more advanced years who exclaims in horror at how late children are dry these days, usually telling the story of their own child (maybe you, maybe your partner) who was dry by six months. Yes, and also reciting the Greek alphabet at nine months and publishing their first thesis on evolutionary theory by the age of fourteen months.

Not.

If this was the case, then this child would have spent their days with a potty gaffer-taped to their bottom. Honestly, believe me – it would not have been physiologically possible for the child to be dry at such an early age (Sorry, Grandma!). What is probably being described is something called reflex training whereby a baby or very young child can be fed and then sat on a potty and some will wee or poo in the potty. But STOP – before you all rush off to reflex train your child, thinking this will put you ahead of the game, it won't. Unless your child has recognized for themselves that they want to go to the toilet, shown that they want to and then taken themselves off (with or without assistance) to go to the toilet, they are not, I repeat *not* toilet/potty trained.

So, rather than rushing to the problem, let's have a quick look at what is realistic in terms of potty training your child. Well, in order for your child to be ready for this process, they have to have an understanding of the physical cues of needing to go to the toilet, and in terms of wanting to urinate this isn't until at least twelve or eighteen months. As far as wanting to poo goes, between the ages of eighteen to thirty months your child will let you know that they have a dirty nappy (although it's not as if you can't tell!). Developmentally it usually goes like this: at approximately eighteen months old a child can hold urine for short periods of time; most children are dry in the day by two years old, and virtually all children aged three; most children are dry at night by the age of three; most children do not soil themselves between the ages of three and four; girls are usually quicker in learning bladder and bowel control than boys.

The key areas of toilet training are as follows:

1 Bladder control by day
2 Bladder control by night
3 Bowel control

However, before we look at how to deal with any problems you may have in one or all of the above areas, let's look at the principles of good potty training.

Successful potty training

It is really your decision whether you go straight to the toilet or use a potty first. Your child may show a preference by trying to climb on a sibling's potty or leap like a daredevil onto the toilet seat. Nowadays there is such an amazing array of equipment for this job! I suggest that if your child goes straight onto the toilet you make sure there are safe little steps for them to climb up and rest their feet on and probably a loo-seat insert. I remember once at a dinner party the small dripping child of my host coming in to demand who took their special seat off the toilet.

Most parents will introduce the potty anywhere between eighteen months and two-and-a-half years. Any time before that is a waste of time because your child will not be physically mature enough to really know when their bladder needs emptying. Most children are daytime trained by thirty months whereas night-time training can range from eighteen months old to five years plus. When you decide to train is very much a decision you must take with an understanding of your child and I would suggest using the following markers as an indication that they might be ready:

They are increasingly independent and want to do things themselves, including trying to dress, taking their trousers and pants down.
They can process and follow simple instructions.
They can walk and sit down well and their balance and co-ordination is good.
They might want to watch you or others on the toilet and pretend to go themselves or pretend via play.
They will have clearly defined periods (three or four hours) when they are dry and then when they are urinating they will tell you.
Will say 'poo' when doing it while also grunting or squatting and will request a nappy change once finished.

These are all indications of a level of maturity and understanding that is necessary to accompany successful and happy training.

On the whole, girls train earlier than boys because where you do your wees and poos is a social skill, and female language superiority below the age of five leads to better social skills and hence often earlier training. Also, it is good to note that if you and/or your partner were late to be trained in this area either by day or night, there will be a significant chance that your child will be too – that's no indication of being flawed or a failure, that's just the way it is for your family.

Before we get to the problem-solving section I think it would be helpful to summarize the golden rules for training your child:

1

Timing is everything. Come to potty training at a time that feels right for you and your child – not because your friend's child of the same age is already trained. So absolutely do not start your child too early. As a trial run you could start in the summer when potties can go in the garden and accidents can be tolerated alongside little ones running around happily with no pants on (another great photo to be shown at the twenty-first birthday!).

2

Be positive and relaxed. You are not in a race, nor need to prove to the world that you are a good parent and your child a developmental genius via their ability to use the potty or toilet – early bladder and bowel training is not an indication of a future place at Oxford University. Be relaxed, calm and positive about toilet training – take it at your child's pace and just don't compare your child to others and get anxious if they are taking longer to train – all children are different and learn at different times and at different rates. Do not be negative about smell, and, if your child wants to proudly show you what they have done, celebrate it! If you are anxious about your child's toilet training, so will they be and this will have a negative impact on their learning plus potentially push you both into the fight or flight situation where toilet training becomes a battleground or you both just give up. And when you are feeling anxious that your child will never be clean just think about how many fifteen-year-olds are still wearing nappies – it'll happen eventually and quicker if you approach it calmly.

3

Reward what you want; ignore what you don't want. As your child shows an interest in using the toilet/potty you can gently prompt them when you think they might be ready to go. Do not over-prompt as this will increase anxiety. Every time your child successfully uses their potty or the toilet praise them as much as you can – the reward will strengthen the behaviour and make it more likely to happen again. Accidents will happen – they are part of learning and so make no great fuss or comment, just wipe up and move on. Do not think you have to explain to your child that they've made a mistake – the positive reinforcement of the correct potty behaviour is enough to increase its frequency. Be matter-of-fact about accidents and give them very little attention; recognize that having accidents is part of learning to stay dry and clean, so do not chastise your child.

4

Learn to sit on the toilet and potty. Before your child can or should be expected to do their wee and poo in a toilet or a potty, they need to understand the principle of sitting on it. Up until now they've had a great time with just having to do their business in a nice warm and encasing nappy with a really very nice parent or carer to wipe their bum and let them go on their merry way. Now suddenly all this has changed and it certainly feels weird sitting with no pants on over this hole with a number of adults smiling and cheering around them – very odd and also a bit breezy! So initially let your child sit on the loo or the potty with their nappies on and just allow them to understand how they are being a clever big boy or girl. If, randomly, they poo or wee in their nappy while sitting there – hurrah! Lots of praise to ensure a strong positive connection is made between sitting on this bizarre seat with a hole in it and doing my poo and wee.

5

Have fun. As with everything else we've looked at so far, the best approach when teaching a child any new skill is to have fun. So, although it may sound odd for me to encourage play in the bathroom and songs and stories while your little one uses the toilet, it really helps to make toilet time fun. If your child is over three, a sticker chart may be a good incentive – a star for every wee – however, if there is an accident, just ignore this. Cuddles and a big family cheer around the toilet work wonders for your child's learning. Also, to help your little chap to learn a good aim, drop three ping pong balls of different colours into the toilet and award points for hitting each one – a competition with Dad always gets those wees in the right place!

Get layering. This is not a psychological perspective but just a great tip I was given when my children were night training. Make up your child's bed with two or three alternate layers of plastic sheet and then cotton sheet and so on. This way any accidents require a simple rip off of the top two layers, a quick change of night clothes and all back in bed without too much fuss.

Monitor the problem

As we have by now well established in other sections of the
book, it is always extremely helpful to monitor the problem
behaviour before trying to tackle it. Keeping a diary of your
child's wetting and soiling will enable you to notice any patterns
in their behaviour and also your responses and how these might
be linked. You might find that there are specific triggers that will
help you predict when wetting or soiling is likely, and so enable
you to gently prompt your child and help them learn to recognize
when they need to use the toilet. Most importantly, you need
to really look at your own emotional state when you are dealing
with your child's toileting behaviour and recognize how far your
anxiety about the whole situation is causing your child to feel
worried and stressed and so wet themselves or retain their urine
until they can wee in their nappy in peace away from you. As
we all know, when we are anxious we automatically want to go
to the toilet, so to introduce anxiety into this area of your child's
learning is clearly counterproductive on many levels. Also, on a
very simple behavioural level, what do you give your child more
attention for – going to the toilet or having an accident?

Day, date and time	Wet or soil?	Where did it happen?	What did your child do?	What did you do?	Outcome

You will find a diary like this in the back of the book – it is the simplest of all diaries and just requires you to be detailed in your recording. Note your child's behaviour prior to the accident: did they look like they knew that they needed the toilet? Do they have a special place to go and wet or soil themselves, e.g., behind the sofa? Did they tell you what they had done or did you spot it later? Build a comprehensive picture of the difficulties and how your interactions with your child are bound up with them. Decide whether you need to have your child assessed medically. If you feel confident that this is a problem that comes from an anxious and stressed atmosphere that surrounds the whole issue of going to the toilet, then you can change that – and here are the ways you can.

DAYTIME WETTING

Daytime wetting usually occurs alongside night wetting and affects more girls than boys, usually because of them slightly wetting themselves when they are laughing (this is very quaintly called 'giggle micturition').

There can be many reasons for wetting, including simply forgetting to go to the toilet when absorbed in play or an activity; a urinary tract infection; a life event that is emotional such as the birth of a new sibling, a family bereavement or starting school or nursery. Some children wet themselves when they are worried, such as when there are family problems or they are having a bad experience; the wetting could be an important communication. Finally, sometimes children wet by day because they don't fully empty their bladder when they go to the toilet or they have a small functional bladder capacity.

Often children will attempt to stop the flow by crossing their legs or holding their genitals or sitting on their foot and it is important to notice these signs so that you can support them and help them learn:

Have a schedule for reminding them to use the toilet in a patient and relaxed fashion and then when they do go ask them whether they feel the urge to wee and what that feels like. Because we usually want to wee or poo after a meal or a drink you could build this schedule around mealtimes. Let them just sit on the toilet or potty and praise them if they do wee in the toilet, and any accident should be ignored. Start to remind them less frequently and praise all and any times that the child remembers by also telling them how clever they were to remind you! If your child seems stressed even by this expectation, you can just go right back to basics and let them sit on the toilet or potty whenever they feel like it – wee or no wee – just to relax them about the whole sitting-down process. Don't see this as a backwards step, rather as a revision of learning!

If your child needs help learning to hold on to their urine, you can help them learn to wait a bit once they get the feeling that they need to do a wee. Distract them with a game or task but keep an eye on their body language so you can cue them to go and successfully wee in the toilet when they clearly can't hold on any more. By increasing the wait by small time increments you can reduce the number of times your child wets themself by increasing the capacity of the bladder.

For some children the whole issue of the toilet has become one associated with failure and letting their parent down, and occasionally these children don't actually want to enter the toilet. Sometimes it helps to break this pattern by letting the child decorate the toilet in a way that they start to feel it is a room that is also theirs – put their pictures on the wall, buy some fun children's hand wash, give them their own hand towel and flannel and put a stack of their books by the toilet.

For older children (aged five plus) there are enuresis alarms that can be worn on the body and in the pants and go off with the first drop of urine (these are discreet and your child won't suddenly go off like a huge fire alarm). This will jolt your child to then go to the toilet to finish their urination – the ongoing effect is that by drawing the child's attention to the need to wee they learn to recognize the need to go to the toilet and use it. These alarms should be used with professional guidance and the resource list at the end of the book will help with this.

If your child's wetting seems to be linked to other behaviours such as being secretive and wetting in places around the house, it might be linked to emotional issues – in other words the child's behaviour is communicating to you that they are feeling unhappy or unsettled about something. In this case, you need to examine what this could be about and if, for example, it is linked to the birth of a sibling or a death in the family, help your child feel understood and treat them with compassion and lots of loving. See the wetting as a secondary issue that will pass as the child feels their emotional needs are understood. Should you want support with this please refer to the resource list at the back of the book.

NIGHT-TIME WETTING

It is estimated that around one in ten five-year-olds regularly wets the bed. There are various factors that may be involved as causes of night-time wetting:

- An infection that needs assessment by a GP and treatment
- Physical immaturity in the systems required for retaining urine during sleep
- A genetic vulnerability
- Emotional problems, such as feeling anxious or unhappy
- Feeling anxious about wetting at night due to picking up the stress or disappointment in a parent when they discover a wet bed in the morning

For night-time wetting I have always been of the opinion that the best thing to do is nothing, and just let learning happen when it happens. Therefore, if you had a night-dry child who, for whatever reason, suddenly isn't, then be extremely relaxed and put them back into trainer pants and say nothing until the days that the trainer pants begin to be regularly dry. If the child comments on wet pants and looks anxious in the morning, just be completely relaxed with them and tell them that there is no problem. Obviously there are also some common-sense approaches:

Restrict large drinks just before bed. If your child drinks well in the day, they will not become dehydrated in the night, so they won't need litres of liquid before sleep.

Get your child into a routine of going to the toilet before bed.

Maybe put your child back into trainer pants just to take the pressure off and let everyone be calm about the whole situation. Try again when there are a few days of dry trainer pants but in the meantime just be cool, calm and collected about wet pants.

Always be positive with your child even if there is a wet bed – your child must not become paranoid or obsessed with wetting the bed as this will only make it worse.

Praise a dry bed/trainer pants with all the gusto you can, but don't show any disappointment if there is a wet bed the next day.

For children over the age of three use a sticker chart to reward a dry bed alongside the praise but do not remove stickers for wet beds or draw in sad faces or black marks. The night-time fairy is often a real incentive, especially if she leaves a tiny treat under the pillow of a child with a dry bed.

'Lift' your child, i.e., take them to the toilet when you go to bed. This can solve the problem of a wet bed but some have argued that it does nothing but give the responsibility for going to the toilet to the parent and not to the child because the child is woken and does not wake themself, therefore it doesn't actually help with learning.

In answer to this it is also possible to use mattress alarms that will sound as the first drop of urine hits the mattress and enables the child to halt the flow while they make their way to the toilet. The principle is that the child associates the relaxing of the bladder sphincter with being woken up and eventually will be able to do this for themselves if necessary without an alarm. The improvement rate for this approach is very good in older children – see the resource list at the back of the book for further advice.

SOILING

This is the least common toileting problem but usually the one that causes the most concern and distress in parents. The reason for this is the negative stigma associated with poo, and poo smells, and how for some parents (and this might include you) dealing with their child learning to poo in the toilet is a revolting task – the problem is that your child will sense this and poo will become something to be ashamed and possibly afraid of.

Soiling difficulties can be associated with a number of factors:

Poor control of the bowel because of poor training.

Emotional issues that cause the child to seemingly regress to a younger stage of development, which can be symbolized by soiling themselves.

Severe emotional distress, trauma or anger where children soil in bizarre ways – hiding their poo or smearing their poo on walls.

Overflow soiling due to constipation whereby the rectum and colon become blocked by a hard mass of poo and the soiling is evidence of loose and watery poo that overflows around the hard mass. In this case your child may have stomach pains and a swollen abdomen. If you are concerned about this, medical assessment is vital. The causes of constipation could be due to retaining poo because of pain when pooing, because of a fear of pooing, because of not being taught how to poo in the toilet and not wanting to soil or because of a poor diet. A medical assessment will establish whether your child is impacted and, if so, effective treatment can be provided.

Following treatment to clear the bowel, a child may then need some gentle and loving retraining to get over their anxiety of pooing, and so that they don't start to retain their poo again. It is also important to look at your child's diet and make sure it is balanced across the food groups with plenty of fruit, vegetables and fibre as well as good levels of hydration. Any emotional issues need to be thought about very carefully and a professional assessment may also be advisable.

However, for a child with soiling difficulties, whatever the cause, there are things that you can do. Your child may not need a professional assessment and you can achieve good bowel habits by using the following techniques:

1. Get friendly with the toilet/potty. OK, brace yourself. I suggest that you let your child watch you poo (you are their role model). Let that poo seem nice and talk them through the process, let them play in the toilet while you go, let them flush the chain and wave goodbye to your poo. Please don't think I've lost all sense and reason; just think about it – you are making the poo event seem fun and non-threatening. Let them decorate the toilet and make it their room too. Do all of this while putting no pressure on them to poo in the toilet. If you are using a potty for training they can sit on this with a book or toy while you sit on the toilet.

2. Sit on the toilet/potty. Let your child sit on the toilet while you are in there and you can chat, talk, read together. There is absolutely no expectation for them to use the toilet, just to feel relaxed sitting on it. If they do a poo in their nappy while they are sitting on the toilet or just in the bathroom praise them for this and make a positive connection with the action and the place. Similarly, let them sit on their potty whenever they want and praise them for this. It is also a good idea to place some steps for them to put their feet on – make sure their upper and lower legs are positioned at a comfortable right angle to each other. Also, if your child is anxious encourage them to blow bubbles as they sit – this will calm them down and introduce fun to the proceedings.

3. Gradually remove nappy/trainer pants. If your child is very reluctant to stop pooing in their nappy/trainer pants, then I suggest that you take this process slowly as in my experience if you try to force your child to poo into a potty straight away they can begin to withhold, and then you run the risk of constipation (see later). See this behaviour as an anxiety of not having the nappy/trainer pants and an anxiety of sitting and pooing, and desensitize your child to these anxieties over time. The nappy/trainer pants feel warm and containing against a bottom, whereas a huge toilet bowl doesn't, so gradually loosening the nappy/trainer pants over time will reduce your child's dependency on that feeling to be there in order to poo. This means that you should gently encourage your child to just sit on the potty as they poo in their nappy/trainer pants and over time loosen the nappy/trainer pants very gradually until they are sitting on the nappy/trainer pants laid over the potty. From here you can slowly have less and less nappy/trainer pants under them until they will poo on the potty holding the clean nappy/trainer pants, and eventually the nappy will go.

As with all other behaviours associated with your child, the most important aspects of potty/toilet training are that you are:

calm;

consistent in your approach;

ensuring others are consistent in the approach;

accepting of the fact that your child is learning and therefore will have 'accidents';

positive, creative and fun; and

linking positive attention to successful toilet behaviour, and appear entirely unfazed if it does not go according to plan.

FINAL THOUGHTS – WHERE PROBLEMS CAN LEAD

Your child will toilet train when they are ready to, so no matter how hard you push them to train at your convenience, they won't. They will, however, develop problems relating to early pressurized training and that could lead to anxieties and delayed training. Other complications could lead to your child being impacted.

As discussed earlier, *faecal impaction* occurs when a child has become constipated and/or has learned to withhold their poos (because they are anxious about letting them go) and so a mass of faeces builds up and grows into a blockage in your child's bowel. This blockage can cause significant pain and discomfort. Often faecal impaction is missed because a child seemingly is showing watery poo – like diarrhoea. However, this is just faecal overflow running around the blockage. Over time, and if not treated, the blockage can grow and cause physiological problems, not just in terms of constipation, but also 'confusing' the bowel in terms of when it's full (because the faecal mass is located in the bowel) and children then become unable to tell when they want a poo (and in some cases a wee).

A manual examination can often identify an impacted bowel and a combination of laxatives and gentle training will help a child get rid of the faeces and learn to recognize the physiological signs of needing a poo and so toilet train successfully. However, some children may need to be scanned in order to identify impaction and in severe cases the faecal mass may need to be removed operatively.

This is the worst-case scenario and should you have any concerns, visit a GP or paediatrician. However, it is worth recognizing that any child who is pressured to toilet train becomes anxious and runs the risk of withholding their poo, and so could end up in this state. Therefore, whether you are desperate to get your child into the prized nursery and so are in a rush to toilet train or want your child trained because your friend's child is, stop yourself and deal with your own anxiety issues. By nursery age most children have bladder control and can hold their urine for a maximum of two to two and a half hours (a typical nursery session) and, as far as I am aware, early toilet training is not a marker of intellectual genius.

And finally . . .

So there we have it. A behavioural psychology whistle-stop
tour through the most common childhood behavioural issues.
If you have read your problem section and still have some specific
questions, check Part Four where I have a range of questions
and answers – some of which might cover your specific issues.
However, remember every child is unique and responds in their
own individual way to the world around them, so the trick is to
take the principles in these technique chapters and confidently
tailor them to your own child's individual needs.

And, just because you are now able to use some techniques
to shape your child's behaviour positively and are feeling more
in control, please don't close this book and think the job is done.
It isn't.

This is where most parenting books end but I now want to
take you on a further journey where you explore the issues that
might also underpin your child's behaviour problems more
deeply – issues that if not addressed could contribute to you
either not successfully using the techniques and finding that they
fail, or that will bubble up again at a later date and cause any
behaviour progress to be undone.

This may sound daunting but I don't want it to. This should be
the most interesting and liberating part of our journey together –
a journey of discovery that: releases your child from blame; allows
you to look at some emotional issues that get in the way of you
enjoying being a parent; and takes you all onwards into a positive,
strong, loving relationship for life where you can positively and
confidently parent your child – *your way*.

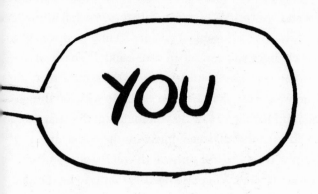

We're now at a stage where the problems are being, or have been, resolved, or you are still struggling to make some positive changes for your child and yourself. Whichever category you fall into, this section is extremely relevant. If you are feeling positive about some effective changes you can see in your child's behaviour, and can feel in the emotional temperature of the family, then the question we now have to ask is: how on earth do we keep things on the straight and narrow? How do you maintain the changes? For those of you who are still struggling with the behavioural difficulties despite trying to use some of the techniques in Part Two, the question is why? What else needs to shift, to be thought about, in order for you to finally get to grips with the difficulties and make some positive and lasting changes.

This part of the book is probably the most unexpected but I would argue the most important. It will cover aspects that other parenting books ignore as they sell in their simplistic notion that parenting is a *job* with a series of techniques that we *do* to our children – that somehow our children can be parented via a series of steps that allows us to be in control. If this was the case, and it was that simple, why in my clinical practice do I meet parents who come to me saying that they've tried every technique under the sun and nothing has 'worked', or that they did manage to shift their child's poor sleeping or eating or behaviour but the changes were short lived and things soon slid back to where they were before? These people are not stupid and it's not as if they aren't trying, because they are and they love their children desperately. Yet, in this age of PARENTING = series of PROBLEMS needing a series of SOLUTIONS they are just not able to make real positive and lasting changes occur.

And why? Because it isn't just about our behaviour as parents, it's about us – who we are and how that significantly impacts on our relationships with our child and consequently on their behaviour.

In this section I will be asking you to honestly look at yourself and think about how your own emotional and psychological nake up is affecting your parenting. This means we will really explore some areas that may feel uncomfortable and could leave you feeling that you are to blame for your child's behaviour difficulties in a big way. So, let me say clearly here and now – this isn't about blame, this is about insight. This is all about understanding your child by understanding yourself. To let go of blame or anxiety or neurosis of any kind and begin to accept your child for who they are and you for who you are. Understanding can be painful but it breeds tolerance, which in turn leads to acceptance and so a more relaxed and intuitive state of loving and nurturing our most precious little people.

Why do I have to think about myself – surely this is about my child?

Yes, you really do! We all, as parents, have to accept the fact that our children's behaviour can only be managed and changed in a positive way if the underlying aspects of those problems are realistically addressed – underlying problems and issues that stem from us.

However, before we launch into all this let me reiterate one thing very clearly: this is not about blame. This is about openly looking at the realities of life – some of which hit, or have hit, some of us harder than others. Consequently, these may have quite a significant impact on our parenting (both positively and negatively) and our child's behaviour (both positively and negatively).

For you to find a confidence in your parenting both now and in the long term, you have to have the courage to look at yourself and question how your emotional and psychological make up is having an impact on your child and their behaviour. Once you have done that, you will not only be able to shift the difficult behaviours that you are dealing with now successfully but also maintain lasting change and develop a positive parent-child relationship for life, one that enables every stage of life and development to be tackled with confidence.

However, I don't want to join the ranks of other 'parenting gurus' by sounding like I am promising a fail-safe approach to the dilemmas and challenges of parenting. As soon as you resolve one challenge, your child will be in a different space developmentally, and presenting you with a different series of challenges. And that's normal – that's the way it should be. Furthermore, you will be at a different time of your life with fresh personal challenges, which will impact both positively and negatively on you as a parent. So let's get real here – being a successful parent is about being able to acknowledge, tolerate and manage the difficulties in a manner that is thoughtful and insightful. Fundamentally, it also means being able to live with the emotional ups and downs, the occasional feelings of hopelessness, helplessness and powerlessness (both for you and your child) that are the realities of parenting, of relationships, of life. It's not about always getting it 'right' or being able to immediately 'fix' things – it's about living through tough times, making mistakes, feeling anxious and unhappy, but underneath it all having an internal core belief that things will resolve in time because the underlying relationship you have with your child and your positive sense of yourself as their parent will see you through.

So, if you want to maintain the changes or if the changes still aren't quite happening, this section will help you think more broadly about your child's behaviour. This is a time to think about the wider issues and find out how far your child's behaviour is reflecting much bigger issues – with you as an adult, with you as a parent, with your partner, or within the family. This section is about understanding our role as parents, and how often the issues are less about our children and more about us. We have to remember to stop using the word 'problem' and recognize that the behaviours you are struggling with as a parent and as a family are communications from your child, who is telling you something about where they are in their life and how they are responding to the way you're responding to them.

You may have read through Part One and looked at your attitude and are now making a supreme effort to respond differently to your child. You may feel more happy and positive about your child, and have implemented some behavioural strategies. But if you are finding that, emotionally, your child can still easily trigger excessive responses and there are times when being consistent or patient is very difficult because the emotion will spill out, then the work that needs to be done now is to think about you. Once you've done that, go back and revisit the earlier sections on how to make the change happen in a way that's positive for everybody.

For example, you might have a child with a sleep problem, and because you wanted to resolve it quickly you tried the rapid-return method but that hasn't worked, and you've now found yourself in a battle of wills with your child. It might be that too much anxiety has built up around bedtime, which you are transferring from yourself to your child. And what you may need to do after reading this section is go back and think about a slower approach, such as the gradual withdrawal. It will take you longer, but may enable your child to overcome the anxiety that has built up around bedtime and you leaving them at that time of the night.

At this stage it is important to really explore your own response to being a parent. Having gone through the process of this book so far, you will likely recognize that your child's behaviour has elicited a vast array of inconsistent responses and sometimes overly emotional responses from you. This is completely natural, but the question you now have to ask is why. Why do I, as the adult, experience such a strong reaction to my child? Why am I behaving like this and what does that tell me about me?

Questions to ask yourself:

- Does my child's behaviour trigger an overly huge emotional response from me at times?
- Are my responses to my child fair in terms of what they have done?
- Does my child 'push my buttons'?
- How far is my child responsible for these buttons existing in the first place?
- Whose issues are they anyway?

The most important thing you can do is understand the fact that when your child elicits these strong emotions from you they are igniting emotional memories of your own experiences of being a child; this is sometimes referred to as your *inner child*. That child is your history and your experiences and your relationships with your parents and your memories of being at school and sleeping in a bed alone and all the things that everyone goes through in life, including moments of total joy and total sadness. We've all had childhoods that have been a mixture of the pleasures of life and the pain of life, some more than others. We must acknowledge that our little children, who probably look quite a lot like us as well, can consciously or unconsciously trigger off a whole raft of feelings associated with what we've experienced in our early life. Unless we can reach this understanding as parents, the chances are we may struggle to create lasting changes.

It's important to remember that you are the adult in the relationship and allow your child to be just that, a child. So, if, for example, you want your child to sleep through the night, you have to, as an adult, stoically get through some sleep deprivation in order to retrain your child. If you give up, and bring the child back in bed with you because you're all so tired, then you're joining them in the place where they don't really understand clearly what they need to do. Unless you can disengage from that kind of response, take a step back and manage it in a way that is responsible, thoughtful and consistent, you will just reinforce the ehaviour – and so the problem continues.

On your child's level the challenges they bring are usually ehavioural, but on your level it becomes incredibly emotional. our emotions then cloud your ability to step back and think, o you know what? We don't want her in our bed any more. e love her, but she's fine and we're just going to have to get her a her own bed. Instead you end up listening to that deep-seated motion that says, 'She'll think we don't love her any more.'

Does the child remain in the parental bed because they cannot e sleep trained and are an impossible sleeper? Or is it because heir progress into their own bed and progress towards good nd healthy independent sleep behaviour is hampered by your ability to step away from your emotional response, which elongs to deep-seated issues inside yourself. Here's an example:

I worked with a family where their five-year-old daughter had been sleeping in their bed since her birth. Initially it was because of ill health but it soon became a massive issue. The parents were unable to move her into her own room and so she was sleeping in the parental bed with her father, and her mother was displaced sleeping in the little girl's bedroom. Try to visualize this – father and daughter in the parental bed together, mother alone in the single bed in child's bedroom next door. I suspect you are seeing an arrangement that has got you thinking beyond the face issue, which is a child not sleeping in her bed. You are probably wondering beyond the child and thinking about the parents and their relationship – just the visual image of them all in their respective sleeping arrangements symbolizing something bigger at work – something embedded in the parental relationship and probably nothing to do with the child, although it is the child who has been labelled as the problem. This type of story will often signal a much bigger issue than a lack of sleep training. These parents had occasionally gone through hellish sleep-training attempts, which had ended in hysterics from the child and arguments between the parents. They were a classic 'we've tried everything but nothing has worked' parental couple.

It was clear that the big mistake they were making wasn't in terms of the techniques they were trying (they could spout them all to me, chapter and verse) but because there had never been any accompanying thinking about how the child ended up in the bed in the first place, how she stayed there and how eventually the mother got kicked out. I have heard this story so many times in slightly different forms – sometimes the child might have been successfully sleep trained only to, a short while later, end up again in the parents' bed. So, for these couples it is very important to have a series of conversations around why that might be. On the surface, it appears to be simply linked with their child and their child's lack of understanding and awareness and not wanting to sleep in their own bed, but underneath it may be that the child is actually being used as a contraceptive, or as a way for the parents to be separate, but in a way that's legitimate and less threatening to their relationship.

For the couple in this example there was a huge backlog of issues to be talked and thought about – painful feelings on both sides that went back to before the daughter was born: the father not wanting to have a child, followed by a physically problematic pregnancy for the mother that was emotionally problematic for the couple. A very difficult, complicated and traumatic birth and an underweight child who spent her first weeks in Special Care led the father to retreat, declaring he'd have nothing to do with any childcare at all (saying he 'didn't do babies') while the mother struggled to cope with a sickly new baby and mild post-natal depression. The father spent an increasing amount of time out of the house and the relationship became strained. Initially it was easier to have the little girl in their bed because she would often be ill in the night. However, as she got older and stronger she still remained there, sleeping down the middle in between her parents. As she began to walk and talk the father became interested in her and began to spend time with her but because he was feeling guilty about his absence when she was ill as a baby, he would allow her to do as she wanted and enjoyed the night times as a time when they could cuddle and bond. The mother would feel annoyed that her husband was so indulgent to the little girl and was also desperate for another child but too afraid to broach the subject because she was both afraid of a negative reaction from her husband and also afraid that she would land up in the same place with another new baby and no support from a man that 'didn't do babies'.

There was a lot of anger and a lot of tears. There was also a lot of courage and honesty from a man who coped with his intense fear that his wife or child would die and so retreated. His wife spoke openly about how she felt rejected by him initially when he wasn't there in the early days but doubly so when he became so infatuated with his daughter almost at the expense of his wife. By looking into both of the parents' histories we could all see why it was so difficult to discuss painful feelings.

I've worked with families where there are unresolved issues about having further children or there are relationship issues that make it hard for a couple to share a bed together. It's easier for them to have a child in their bed, even if they then subsequently label that child as the problem. Take the child out of the bed, and then the whole thorny issue of intimacy or further children raises its head: 'Oh my gosh – panic, panic, panic – don't want to deal with this, don't want to look at it' – allow the child back in. And this was how it was for the family in my example until they bravely addressed their past and present issues and freed their little girl up from having to divert attention away from such painful things via her behaviour.

As soon as they started talking to, and understanding and forgiving, each other it took one night (and 297 returns) to sleep train their lovely daughter.

Questions to ask yourself:

- Could your child's behaviour be helping 'solve' other bigger issues that are not to do with them?
- If you made positive changes to your child's behaviour, would you find other emotional difficulties would open up?
- Should children be the cement in families and relationships where there are other issues to be resolved?

So my child's behaviour could be a symptom of other issues that are not necessarily to do with them?

Exactly! Be prepared to look beyond your child's behaviour and think about what it is showing you that might be going on elsewhere in these very intense and emotional relationships within the family and the extended family. If you don't, then you may be able to superficially change their behaviour problems for a short time, but there won't be long-term positive change because the underlying issues, the issues that fed into the problems in the first place, will resurface. This is why a problem/solution-focused approach to parenting isn't enough, because your child will have a sleep problem for a reason, or isn't eating for a reason. There is an underlying cause for why potty training has become a stressful nightmare, or the tantrums just go on and on and on. And these reasons must be addressed alongside the practical aspects of the problem resolution.

Therefore, in my example family and maybe this might be the same for yours, the child's behaviour problems were used as a crutch for enabling the family to function more efficiently and not argue and fall apart. The little girl enabled her parents not to have to be alone and intimate with each other, thus avoiding their issues relating to sex and having other children – issues that were huge and weighted in emotion. In effect, this little girl was the cement in her parents' fragile relationship because by allowing them not to talk about their problems legitimately (because it was her 'fault' being so difficult at bedtime) she enabled a peace (albeit uneasy) to be maintained.

So, if there *are* much bigger underlying issues, such as marital issues, or relationship problems amongst other members of the family, these can be left unaddressed as the family focuses on the behaviour of the child. A family can find it far less threatening to keep the status quo in this way, rather than look beyond their child's behaviour and take ownership of their own issues and difficulties and risk big arguments and potential rifts.

This broader understanding of the little girl's behaviour comes from taking a ***systemic view***. What this means is that we have looked outside and beyond the child's problem behaviour and thought about what the behaviour means in terms of the overall functioning of the bigger picture – the family and often beyond. I am going to continue this systemic thinking as I ask you to be very honest with yourself while you read on and think beyond your child's behaviour. Think about how it relates to other underlying issues that belong not to the child but maybe to you, your partner and other members of the child's immediate support system.

Furthermore, consider this: if your child's behaviour does represent both other issues and is also maintained or keeps relapsing because of these issues, then your child is doing you and the family a huge favour. I know this sounds completely bizarre but in essence your child's behaviour is highlighting that there are other underlying problems that need to be thought about and, in effect, it is your child who is honestly representing how people are feeling. Therefore, not only is your child the most honest in the family system but also paradoxically the one that is bringing some difficulties to light and helping the family, or individuals within the family, to address some bigger issues.

Questions to ask yourself:
- If you take your focus away from your child's behaviour and look at others within the family network, do you see other issues?
- Could your child's behaviour be a reflection of some or all of those issues?
- Is your child's behaviour their means of communicating what they feel and sense around them?

Are your child's problems the best thing that could happen to you and your family?

Hmmm. An interesting, surprising and rather strange thought!

Having spent many years working with children and families, one of the key strategies that I use on meeting a family for the first time is that I will shake the hand of the child or the young person who is being identified as being the problem before anyone else in the family, even their parents. This may seem odd, and in fact many families look quite shocked, but while I am shaking this child's hand, I am also congratulating them for bringing their family to a place where everyone can sit down and have a series of conversations that are less angry, less full of blame and are more constructively focused on trying to understand how the family has reached a stage of crisis. The message I am giving to them and to you, to a greater or lesser degree, is that your child's behaviour is actually communicating that there are bigger problems within the family system and these problems need to be addressed.

Rather than being the identified and defined problem, the child is reflecting issues within the bigger system. And by developing this systemic awareness – the awareness of your child's role within the system within which they live – you're making your child the communicator rather than the perpetrator of the problems. This thinking and understanding will herald a very significant and positive shift.

A good place to begin is by reflecting on the family structure and what that tells you about other underlying family issues that could be contributing to the problems.

Questions to ask yourself:
Should you stop identifying your child as the real problem?
Has your child enabled you to begin to think more widely about problems and difficulties that exist?
Given limited verbal ability, does your child communicate their responses to the family atmosphere most efficiently via their behaviour?

Family structure

A useful exercise to help you think about the relationships within your family is to find a photograph of each member of your family, and your extended family (grandparents, aunts, uncles, cousins, etc.), if they are also embedded in the problems that you are having with your child.

Sitting at a table, arrange these photographs in a way that you think reflects the structure of your family as if you were hanging them on the branches of a tree. One way of doing this is to think about who you perceive as being the most powerful person in your family (put them at the top of the tree), and then the next powerful, and so on, down to who is the least powerful.

If you think that there are two people who have an equal amount of power, then put them next to each other – on branches that are on the same level. So this is like a family tree, but representing power rather than age. Think, also, about the spaces between the different family members – if some are closer, represent that by placing their photos nearer to each other.

The next step is to look at your 'family tree' and try to work out why it has grown like this. In a healthy functioning family, I would be looking for the adult or adults who are the main carers or parents to be side by side at the top, heading up the other members of the family system. In a traditional nuclear family, for example, you would have Mum and Dad next to each other and then, below them, the two, three or four children together on an equal level. Include extended family as relevant and position them in terms of distance and height to reflect their influence on your core family.

Often when I do this exercise with families, the child with the behaviour problem is placed at the top of the family structure, giving them the most power, and parents put themselves below because they feel powerless in the face of their child's behavioural difficulties. If you are now looking at your family photos and you can see the power being held by your child at the top, before you begin to resent them, or feel sorry for yourself in this powerless position, ask yourself how it has come to this.

Children who are very powerful can often feel very uncomfortable with their influence, and, in my experience, will up the ante with their behaviour because they are actually asking for somebody to set a boundary, for someone to take charge, for someone to show them what they need to do, and to help them learn when what they are doing isn't right. The less children are contained, and the less children are given clear and consistent messages about their behaviour, the more they will behave in a way that seems out of control and powerful, because they are asking to be helped and understood.

As well as looking at your child and where they are in the family structure and what that means, also look at yourself, your partner, the other children, as well as other family members. Does the family feel balanced? If you are parenting with a partner, are you side by side or does one of you appear higher up in the structure – having more power and control? Are there other extended family members who have become too involved in your core family structure, maybe an in-law who has a huge amount of influence? Do you see groups forming within the family, such as one parent having the children nearer to them than the other?

It might also be helpful to replicate this exercise with photos of yourself as a child and your parents/siblings. See how far your current family structure reflects the family structure you came from as a child. It may be very similar, or perhaps it is the reverse of what you experienced, because you are trying so hard to correct difficulties and issues that you had as a child. An example might be that in your family as a child you came near the bottom and always felt dominated and controlled. However, in your core family now you see your child at the top partly because you've not wanted them to feel dominated and so have given them a lot of power (to compensate for what you felt about how it was to be a child). Also, they're possibly in control because you automatically assume a submissive position based on how you felt growing up.

In this scenario my hunch would be that your powerful child acts out and becomes wilful and dominating, which you then find hard to manage. It also makes you very angry as feelings of powerlessness from your own childhood bubble up. The past and the present are colliding in a problematic and difficult way.

Being a parent is about finding a balance in all things, and in finding that balance sometimes we over- and sometimes we under-parent, but this should generally only be because we are genuinely feeling our way through our role as a parent and not because we are trying to compensate for our own issues and our own histories. This is incredibly difficult and not always possible, because we cannot help but be a product of where we have come from and what we have experienced. However, if we have insight into this, we become more able to stop ourselves when we are replicating patterns or trying overly hard to correct previous family issues. Or, if we can't stop ourselves but can recognize what our behaviour has represented, we can then find a way of communicating that to our child so our child understands we may have made a mistake and we are sorry: that is all part of the important lessons that children need to learn to survive in this world.

Questions to ask yourself:

Are you seeing family relationships that are imbalanced?

Can you see how your approach to parenting is affected by your own childhood experiences?

Are you unconsciously trying to compensate for feelings about how you were parented?

So is it all lost because we're going to mess our kids up anyway, given the fact that we all come with histories and baggage?

Life isn't about getting it right and living in a sanitized problem-free manner. We are all products of our past and this, fundamentally, makes us who we are. Life isn't about erasing the past – it's about learning from it, learning to live with it and moving on from it and there is nothing that requires us to do this more than having our own children.

Exploring our pasts, we are, in therapeutic language, examining our own personal *trans-generational patterns* of feelings, behaviours and relationships. These are patterns of relationships that flow down from generation to generation, family to family. You may have caught yourself saying to your partner or observing to your friend how 'I sounded just like my mother' or 'you sounded just like your father' and that may be said in a positive or in a critical, negative and disparaging way.

Often we become so aware of the issues of our own childhood that we are unhappy with, particularly when we have our own children, that we will do everything in our power not to replicate them. In doing so, we can move too far in the other direction. Try to be very honest with yourself about whether what you are communicating to your child and the way you are behaving with them reflects a time in your life or issues in your relationships and early years that have nothing to do with your child.

We thought earlier about a family tree where you place yourself at the bottom of the family relationships and your child at the top - a situation that reflects a child with more power than the parent. This might reflect itself, for example, if you can't set a boundary with your children and possibly that is because when you were a child you were brought up by a parent who was so strict and repressive that for you to be assertive about your own wants and needs has always been very difficult. And so now as a parent when you do try to say no and your child reacts very normally, that is, pleads and cries and tries to get their own way, you don't see a toddler having a tantrum because they can't get their own way but a small person in acute emotional meltdown that may lead to long-term damage. Your perception of your child's behaviour in the moment then is coloured by your own emotional memory of what it felt like to be small and have a very dominant person saying no.

In your childhood maybe the authority was overused and too repressive and has left you insecure about being clear and assertive and also easily manipulated by your child's resistance to the boundaries you set as a parent because you react so emotionally to their response, become anxious (the fight/flight response) and either get locked into a battle with them (fight) or cave in (flight). The anxiety linked to your childhood experiences pollutes your parenting of your child and they do not get clear or consistent parenting.

Questions to ask yourself:

Do you find parenting a challenge because you don't know what
'to do' in terms of responding clearly to your child?
Or – do you find parenting a challenge because your emotions
get in the way of your responses?
Are your perceptions of your child's behaviour distorted by your
emotional responses that come from how you felt as a child?

Projection

Moving on with our thinking we are now really getting to grips
with the notion that it isn't just our behavioural responses to
our child that affects their behaviour but the emotional content
of that response. These emotions are known as *projections* –
feelings from within us that are linked to our own pasts and
histories, which we then project onto our child. In effect, our
child becomes a receptacle for our own emotions and issues –
we emotionally dump on them while all they are doing is
responding as a child who is developing and learning the rules
of the game (life).

In Part One I asked you to make a list of the positives and
negatives about your child. Now make a list of the positive aspects
of going through this process as you are trying to resolve their
difficult behaviours. Look at it closely and notice other difficult
things that are now coming out. If, for example, your child is
now eating well at the table, has that left any other difficulties
for you to deal with? For example, issues within yourself or your
relationship – just like our earlier example of the couple who,
once their daughter left their bed and they were both in it
together again, had to address the really big issues between them.
So, are you now left with an understanding of your own neurosis,
which has left you feeling quite uncomfortable? These are the
feelings that were being previously projected onto your child, but
now you are holding on to them and taking responsibility for

them so your little one can carry on and be the child. It feels tough but is an essential part of parenting – not using your child as your emotional outlet. You are tolerating the difficult feelings as an adult and not making them your child's problem.

When you find yourself in a situation with your child where you acknowledge that their behaviour is stirring up such intense emotions in you, try to step back and begin to adopt an ability to question yourself and your own behaviour. In doing that, you will start to build an awareness of how your own emotional issues are being keyed into by your child – many people would say that their child 'knows which buttons to press'. These buttons are our insecurities and emotional vulnerabilities. Is it fair to blame a child for pushing them? Do we honestly believe that they are scheming in their little mind to get what they want by really stressing us out? No, they have learned, because we have taught them by our responses, that certain behaviours of theirs present us with the greatest problems, and in those situations we are likely to give them the most attention, give in, etc. In times like these it is easy to take those emotions and push them back out on to your child and make your child responsible for them. This is projection.

So, my child puts their banana in the video player: it's irritating, and they know they shouldn't do it, but actually they are two and a half, and the only way they are really going to learn is by pushing boundaries – being a child – and getting consistent messages. However, because I've told them fifteen times not to put their banana in the video player, yet they repeatedly do it, I eventually become hysterically angry with them. I might scream at them, tell them I wish I'd never had them, even smack them and be angry with them for the rest of the day. When my partner comes home, I might say, 'You deal with them! I don't want to know them any more!'

This is a huge emotional response, which reinforces the behaviour on a behavioural level because you're giving it so much attention. On an emotional level it pushes and squashes intense emotions that belong to you, an adult, into this small person, who didn't consciously trigger them in you and who has no ability to filter them out.

How do you see yourself as a parent?

The situation above is an example of a mismatch of behaviour and interpretation of behaviour. Such a projection comes from your own fundamental belief systems about yourself as an adult. If you believe you are a failure, perhaps, or not good enough, or even worthless; if you look at yourself in the mirror and you don't like who you see, you label yourself in a negative way, are apologetic or have little sense of self-esteem or even just have the bog-standard guilt that most parents carry around with them, then the moment your child does something wrong, or something that embarrasses you, or keys into that sense of 'I'm a failure' or 'I'm out of control' or 'I am a terrible parent – look how they are behaving and it's all my fault' or 'I'm not here enough', then you will go into meltdown. It becomes about you, when actually children are supposed to make mistakes. If your child's mistake compounds your negative beliefs about yourself, which are in turn linked to your own childhood or difficulties in your life and relationships, the messages you have been given in life by your parents, carers, teachers, partner, etc., then your child is going to find themselves in the path of a huge response that is completely mismatched to their behaviour.

Behaviourally, you are reinforcing their behaviour so they're more likely to do it, but also on a more emotional level, by projecting your feelings of worthlessness onto your child, you are likely to cause them then to develop into the same adult as you, with similarly negative self-beliefs. This brings us back to the concept of trans-generational patterns – patterns of emotional distress and dysfunctional behaviour that traverse through families because one generation projects it onto the next. It's a very, very powerful process within relationships.

It is easy to fall into the trap of pushing our anger, sadness, pain, frustration and stress out and onto our children, and make them responsible for it, rather than really take responsibility for these feelings ourselves, and take a close look at what these feelings are about.

Projection comes in many forms, not only from generation to generation. I've worked with children who have had an elder sibling who's died either at childbirth or following childbirth. Then this child comes along and either they are a disappointment because they're the wrong gender or they're so wrapped in cotton wool because of the parents' understandable deep grief with the loss of their baby. I will very gently help the parents reflect on the fact that this little child they are experiencing difficulty with has been made responsible for, and had projected onto them a huge amount of emotional baggage that has nothing to do with them at all.

But you must be asking yourself, how can I be rational, try not to project my feelings, when I just feel so emotional? It's not possible to take emotion out of parenting, and nor would we want it to be. But, if you need to make a decision about something that is very difficult, the more you can take emotion out of it, the more clarity you'll have in your thinking.

Once you can stand back and rationalize it in that way, you then need to ask *why* does it drill into me to such a degree that I want to get down on the floor and join them in their tantrum. We all have so much pressure crammed into our lives, our days are often scheduled so carefully, that there is no room for anything spontaneous. Particularly something spontaneous that might derail the train that just has to go down the track otherwise everything else will fall apart. When you are responding to your child with a huge amount of emotion and anger, recognize that you're probably stressed, you're probably tired, you're probably doing too much yourself and expecting too much of your child. At a time when you are calm start on this journey of reflection and explore the moments that bring out such overwhelming emotions. Use this opportunity to reflect on your own issues, both past and present, in order to separate them from your child so that you can successfully navigate your child through their own development without polluting them with issues from yours that they have no responsibility for.

Questions to ask yourself:
Does your child receive way more negative emotion from you than their behaviour deserves?
Is your child at times the receptacle for your other insecurities, stresses, frustrations, long-term issues?
Are you likely to overwhelm and confuse your child and so push them into the same emotional space as you?

When projection becomes overwhelming

Sometimes there are life experiences that cause us such huge emotional and psychological challenges that it is very difficult to avoid projecting how we are feeling onto and into our child – these may be situations, events or experiences that link to the past or to the present. These projections may need more than just a series of conversations with yourself, friend or partner. They may require some professional support to enable you to really disentangle yourself from a genuine difficulty separating your child from yourself when it comes to the overwhelming feelings you experience as their parent. As a way of understanding these more extreme situations we'll consider post-natal depression and abuse in childhood.

PROJECTIONS FROM THE PRESENT – POST-NATAL DEPRESSION

After having a baby many women experience a short period of mild depression called 'the baby blues'. However up to 10% of new mothers go on to develop post-natal depression (PND) or post-natal illness (PNI), and research indicates that only one in four will seek help – usually because many women feel so ashamed that they are a bad mother (they aren't) and are frightened that their child will be taken away from them (it won't). PND usually emerges within the first year after birth (often when the baby is between four and six months) and the rate of its onset and severity can vary from woman to woman. The common signs are extreme tiredness; a lack of motivation; feeling helpless, hopeless, guilty and inadequate, particularly about not loving the baby or being a 'good enough' mother; irritability; problems with appetite, sleeping and sex drive; anxiety, paranoia, possibly experiencing panic attacks, problems with concentration and decision making; and sometimes thoughts about self-harming and suicide. All these thoughts and emotions are very frightening and many women feel out of control, ashamed and guilty, particularly as they feel that they are supposed to be feeling immense joy at having their new baby.

Having PND *does not* mean you are a bad mother – it is an illness that is treatable and happens because of a variety of causes that vary between individuals. These causes include a lack of support, the shock of birth and motherhood, other life stresses, childhood experiences and possibly because of the huge hormonal changes after the birth and, for some, the body not adjusting well to this. A key fact is that it is impossible to predict whether you will get it again if you have another child and sometimes mothers can experience PND following the birth of their second child having not experienced it first time round.

It is important to seek help because, as with any illness, the longer it is left untreated, the worse the PND will get. With the courage to speak about how they are feeling, women with PND can then access support from family and health professionals, and get the effective treatment available. Treatments include counselling, psychotherapy and prescription medications, e.g., antidepressants, which are not addictive and some can be taken safely while breastfeeding. Also, some mothers with PND have found complementary and homeopathic therapies very helpful to support the pathway to feeling and being well again. As a final note, I have heard some fathers describe symptoms similar to PND following the birth of their child and would encourage them to seek help for how they are feeling in the same way.

I worked with a mother once who was depressed and so had

never bonded with her youngest child, her daughter. The little girl was having huge tantrums, which were in part about a lack of boundaries but were also closely linked to the fact that she had never really been nurtured from being a baby. Her tantrums were literally like those of a newborn baby. Every time the little girl had a screaming tantrum, I asked the mum to get down on the floor and rock her, a kind of regression therapy. Ignoring the tantrum would've been the worse thing she could do, but it was only by being aware of her own depression that we could understand how to approach her daughter's behaviour.

PROJECTIONS FROM THE PAST – ABUSE
Abuse, whatever form it takes, can live on until it is addressed and processed – I have worked with adult survivors of familial abuse who continue to live within abusive relationships (either as abuser, the abused or both) and replicate the destructive patterns over and over again either towards their partners or their children.

To be abused as a child violates a person not only physically but also emotionally. It can leave children and the adult survivors with significant problems forming safe and nurturing relationships, as their early and key experiences crossed and shattered the appropriate and necessary boundaries that exist within relationships and enable healthy trust and dependence. Thinking about behaviour from a systemic standpoint as we have earlier, we can see that abuse causes the boundaries between relationships to be blurred, overstepped and torn down. A healthy family structure comprises a parent or parents who work together to lead the family in a nurturing and containing manner. The boundary between parent and child is one that exists in order to enable the establishment of the safe and non-threatening authority that is central to effective and loving parenting. Boundaries are necessary in all systems (for example in the workplace, in sports teams, as well as in the family) in order for people to coexist in a way that respects each other's needs and allows the system to function effectively and safely. Of course, tensions exist within all systems, and especially within families at times, and this is normal. However, such tensions would be managed by the family relationships (and the appropriate boundaries between those relationships) so emotional difficulties do not escalate out of control, arguments do not become destructive and problems can be heard and managed in a supportive way.

There is a clear line to be drawn here and if you were beaten as a child you don't want to beat your child. If you were abused as a child you don't want to abuse your child. I have worked with parents where they've had really, really traumatic childhoods and will go one way or the other, they'll either repeat the abuse or they will overcompensate.

As an example, I once worked with a family where the woman was terribly abused by her father and her brother. She went on to marry a kind and loving man and they had a daughter and a son. The problem was that the daughter slept in the mother's bed, because, as much as she loved her husband and her son, she just couldn't trust them. She was holding on to a great deal of pain and fear, and had never been able to tell her husband about her childhood abuse. It was relatively easy to get their daughter out of her parent's bed but after a while the mother became depressed. She did seek treatment, though, and gradually she was able to heal, so in a roundabout way her child had helped her.

Questions to ask yourself:
- Is your child's behaviour a reflection of the pain you carry from past or present very emotionally, psychologically and possibly physically negative experiences?
- Should you blame your child for their difficulties when in essence they are only reflecting yours?
- Should you blame yourself for your difficulties that were or are very much overwhelming you and outside of your control?

Seeking help

If your behaviour towards your child is becoming outside your control, if you know you don't want to be responding or behaving in the way that you are, or you feel uncomfortable and lie awake at night thinking about it, then seek help. Go and talk to someone who is detached from your life but has the training to help you analyse what has led you to this place. They can help you then to separate your emotional debris from this little person who did nothing more than set off a memory or issue in you – who inadvertently pressed the buttons. See page 228 in the Resources section.

Questions to ask yourself:

Is seeking help an admission of failure?

Is seeking help a reflection of courage and strength?

Is seeking help a priority for you and your child at present?

Separating our children from our issues

So we have come to the stage where we can acknowledge that our response to our child is made up of everything that makes us who we are and can reflect our emotional baggage and issues. This baggage comes from our pasts, our parents' pasts and so on – dripping through generation by generation. We need to think about our child's behaviour and accept the fact that they are a product of a wider system that has a huge amount of emotion floating around it. We are then at times projecting our stuff onto our kids and by doing so turning their normal toddler/young child behaviour into a huge deal and so making it into problem behaviour. Projection is a bit like kicking the dog when you're down. When you feel frustrated, children can be the receptacle that we pour our emotional 'stuff' into. It happens. We all do it – we're human beings. The important thing is to catch yourself when you see it, and don't be afraid to say sorry.

Should we all just descend into a pit of despair and accept that our poor children will be emotionally scarred by us forever? No! What we are learning is not only important in terms of our insight and understanding of ourselves, allowing us to step back and prevent some of our overly emotional responses from getting in the way of our parenting, but also helping our children learn from us and our mistakes in order to be prepared for the tough world that we all live in.

'Mummy was really grumpy earlier, and I was cross with you when you didn't eat nicely at the table, but I shouldn't have yelled like that. And I'm sorry I made you feel scared and you cried and you saw me crying. I love you. Let's have a nice cuddle and be friends again. It doesn't take away the fact that Mummy's cross about what happened at the table, but I think the way I got cross really upset you and I'm sorry about that.'

Being a parent is a learning ground for so many things, and it's important as parents that, if we feel that we've gone too far and got really angry, we can go to our children and apologize. We can't get through life and not make mistakes, but it's about having the courage to be able to recognize them and having the courage to be able to say sorry. That's what relationships are: you fall out, and become friends again. Unless children can see this dynamic in the safe family unit, they are going to be completely ill-equipped for life, where people do get stressed and angry and cross and project things. But when you're two or three or four, and you're still trying to make sense of the world, obviously your parent having a huge emotional response to you is something that is going to be very tricky and difficult to understand.

Questions to ask yourself:

Do 'perfect' parents and families set children up with unrealistic expectations about life and relationships?

Is it wrong to make mistakes and then say sorry to our children?

How far do you blame yourself for being flawed – for being a human being?

Multiple projections – mixed messages

What happens when there are many projections within a family – for example from you and from your partner? Your child brings up feelings and issues in both of you and so here we have a situation where the child themselves gets confusing messages because of your differing responses to them and to each other.

I worked with a family where the parents had two older boys and one very precious younger girl. These parents had been desperate for a girl and so she was adored to the point of becoming incredibly spoilt and demanding, hiding the lovely little person she was inside. This little girl hit her mother when she was angry, and her mother would be quite cross about that, and so try to discipline her. But the father would just say, 'No, no, no don't shout at her, it's fine,' and then, of course, Mum would resent Dad and they'd get into a circle of resentment that had absolutely nothing to do with their daughter. When we talked it through the mother asked, 'Why is it OK for her to hit me?' and he would say, 'Well, she's angry.' 'Yes, but she's *hitting* me. You really don't respect me. If you respected me, you wouldn't allow this to happen. And, by the way, you don't show me respect about x, y, z and about five hundred other things…'

Suddenly their child's behaviour was an embodiment of a much bigger issue about respect. And meanwhile the little girl was getting very mixed messages. Her behaviour was escalating as she began to exploit the split between her parents' management of her, in order to get what she wanted (they gave her permission to do this via their lack of unity and consistency in their parenting of her).

Within families you find that sometimes parents or carers who are working as partners or within extended families where grandparents may also be care givers, children can get very mixed messages because each adult is projecting onto that child their own feelings and issues about themselves and about their relationship with each other. So the child gets a number of messages, and therefore ends up confused and unclear about what is expected of them. It is no surprise, therefore, that their behaviour will often escalate and become out of control.

It was important with this family for Mum and Dad to come together about their daughter's behaviour and agree on their responses. So hitting was out, they agreed, and they would begin to show a strong, united front together. This meant their daughter was very cross and bewildered at these new parents she couldn't play off against each other, and so her parents had to stand firmly together. Whenever they had any issues with each other, whether the mother felt the father was being too indulgent and soft, or the father felt his wife was becoming too disciplinarian, they had to discuss these feelings away from their child. But the next question was how Mum and Dad could talk through their own issues about respecting each other and so deal with the bigger, long-term picture.

Questions to ask yourself:
How often does your child get mixed messages about their behaviour? How far do those messages reflect other people's issues and concerns? How far does this confuse and unsettle a child and what impact is this likely to have on their behaviour?

How we can give mixed messages

If you're at all ambivalent about the approach you are taking with your child's behaviour, then you may fall into the trap of giving out mixed messages. Monitor yourself and you may find that one day you're one thing, and the next another. Or you'll look at them in a certain way but what you're saying and what you're projecting with your body language is completely different. Or, if you're parenting with a partner, you find yourselves contradicting each other.

Sometimes it's simply that you haven't talked or thought it through. You haven't set the ground rules. Parenting is an emotional experience; it's a journey for parents as much as the children, but it's a practical experience as well. And we need to find a balance between being strategic and thoughtful, and spontaneous and emotional. We have to allow ourselves to accept that sometimes we're going to make mistakes and allow our emotions to cloud our actions – that's life. But we also have to treat the role of parenting with the respect we would treat any other job, which is that we have to think about it and talk about it. And with a clearer strategy there is in turn more room for spontaneity and more tolerance of the things you decide are not so important.

Questions to ask yourself:

- Are you really 100% happy, committed and positive about the approach you are taking to resolve your child's difficulties?
- Is everyone involved in your child's care taking the same approach?
- Does everyone agree on what is acceptable and unacceptable in terms of the behaviour of your child?

Parenting contract

If you and your partner can now accept and own the fact that
who you are as individuals and parents is a melting pot of
different feelings, emotions, stresses and pressures of the day,
including your relationship, and your early experiences as
children within your own families, then you now need to think
about ways in which you can define your own parenting strategy
between the two of you. I will often suggest to parents that they
literally write a parenting contract. Sit down together, or with a
friend or other member of your family if you are a single parent,
and look at each and every behaviour that your child does that
challenges either one of you or both of you and discuss very
honestly, without judgement or blame, reasons why these
behaviours might have developed and ways in which you can
try to parent effectively and consistently together.

It may be that sometimes the conversation becomes heated
so you have to agree to take some time out, calm down and then
come back again. It may also be that you start blaming each other
but then you have to revisit the point of the exercise, and that
is to enable your child to feel clear about what you expect from
them so their behaviour is less difficult and problematic for you
and the rest of the family.

Writing this contract may require compromise on both sides,
which is no bad thing, because that's what relationships are
about, and if one of you seems to be dominating or having a
stronger voice in this process then that needs to be addressed
as well, so that the final contract, the final agreement between
the two of you as parents, feels equal and that everybody's
emotional needs are respected and understood.

In emotionally charged moments, you and your partner can
take a step back and look at the contract together to remember
what you agreed when things were less emotional and more
thoughtful, strategic and calm.

Questions to ask yourself:
- Are all adults involved in the care of your child coming from different places because of their own issues?
- Can you agree on the boundaries of your child's behaviour?
- Can you find a way, as adults, to discuss this constructively?

What do you expect from your child?

If you are attempting to have some kind of agreed contract based on your child's behaviour, make sure it is balanced and fair in terms of the expectations you have of that behaviour. I've worked with many families where the expectations placed on the child are so huge that no adult could realize them, never mind a small person. So, when you write your contract, be very careful that it takes into account the realities of what it is to be a young child. Remember that children do have behavioural outbursts – it is part of their learning (and that has to be part of the flexibility that is written into your contract), and is part of your parenting. I have had parents who phone in and say, 'Oh, he just won't eat broccoli.' When I ask if he eats other vegetables and the answer is yes then I have to ask them why they are investing so much emotion in broccoli. Take a view; pick your battles.

I remember a couple who had two children, an elder daughter who had always been relatively easy to parent and a young son who was mischievous and spirited, and caused a huge amount of anxiety for both the parents. When this boy was younger, he would drive his parents up the wall and they would think, Why are you doing that? Your sister would never do that. But they look at him now and realize this was part of his personality that one day will make him an incredibly effective and successful adult. He has a spontaneity that drives them completely mad at times but which is his, and who are they to take it away? The tighter they were squeezing him, the more he was trying to break out, but as soon as they acknowledged that they did need to set boundaries but in a different way, with a real understanding of who he was, and is, it changed.

How you view your child will be based on your many deep-seated beliefs about yourself and others, and on issues that are resolved, partly resolved or unresolved from your early life that are impossible not to project on to your child. There are expectations that come out of all those thoughts and feelings. You might find that your child isn't who you expected, a mini version of yourself. They might be introverted while you are an extrovert. So you wonder, Why aren't they like me? Why aren't they coping in the world? This might set off a cycle of anxiety, which will bring out the extreme extrovert in you, causing your child to withdraw further. Or you're an introvert and your child is much more extrovert. You might find they draw too much attention for comfort and the danger is that a child will then be repressed and squashed, and then they will have to break out with extreme behaviour.

Take a step back and look at your child as a unique individual who has a combination of genetic and environmental influences that make them into the kind of person they are. Make sure that your expectations of their behaviour are matched against who they are and their personality, and not who you want them to be, and your personality.

Questions to ask yourself:
Are your expectations of your child's behaviour appropriate for their age and stage of development?
Do your expectations reflect their needs – or yours?
Are you attempting to mould your child into what you want rather than who they are?

Futuring

This leads into thinking about the concept of *futuring*, where you imagine what this little part of your child's character will enable them to be and do in the future. That flash of independence which is a challenge now means that when your child is beginning to make their own way out in the world, they will have a vital coping mechanism, so it's actually a part of your child being a great person.

I knew a family who had three sons. The middle son was the 'problem' child, and was demonstrating behaviours that were so traumatizing to both parents that the father would often want to leave the house and not come home because he was afraid of his own rage, and how that rage might be taken out on the child. The mother would often sit powerless, weeping in the corner, while this little boy ran roughshod over the whole family.

When I talked to the parents about this child, their beliefs and their expectations of this child, we started to think more specifically about who they thought their son would be when he grew up. What they described to me was a young man, in prison, who had a series of anti-social behaviour orders and convictions, and who, basically, was washed up and a no hoper. It was an extremely powerful image that these parents projected onto their little three-and-a-half-year-old boy, and what it did was set this child up so specifically that there was no way he could be anything other than a child who was out of control, because his parents were imagining him in the same way in his 20s.

This was an extreme example, but we can all be guilty of projecting negative attributes onto children with problem behaviours. Yes, we all want our children to have good manners, to sit nicely at the table, to eat a balanced diet, to sleep well in their own bed and to know that you don't bash people up if you want something, but that you ask nicely. But, if it takes a child longer to learn one thing than another, then think of it as a bit of what makes them their own person coming through. And know that at their eighteenth birthday party when you bring out the photos in front of their friends, it'll be hilarious and you'll look at them and think, I can still see that in you, but now I celebrate it and I love it because it makes you who you are. It's a question of finding a balance and accepting that children are not perfect, and why should they be? We're not! So question yourself when you are thinking about your child's behaviour. Who do you want to change it for? Is your child really a monster? Are they really careering dangerously out of control?

Questions to ask yourself:

- How far are you setting up your child to have long-term problems by the way you are labelling them now?
- Are the behaviours you struggle with possibly emerging character strengths?
- Are you confusing appropriate toddler behaviours with inappropriate adult behaviours and so consigning your child to a lifetime of problems?

Over-parenting

Sometimes we want to manage, change or influence our children's behaviour, not necessarily because it is the best for them but because it is the best for us. In the same way that we may want to drive a car that people look at and think, Ooh, he's got a great car, or wear clothes that make people say, 'Ooh, she's got some style!' – we want people to look at our children and go, 'Wow!' This is natural, but it can lead to over-parenting, where children do every activity, or get everything they want – and they are literally exhausted children, because they are being moulded and shaped into these perfect little examples of how successful we are as parents.

It can be very damaging when we want our children to be a reflection of how we're doing in life. Having a child is the biggest narcissistic trip: you look at your child and think, Look, she's me, he's you, us, aren't they wonderful? If we load up too much on our children in terms of what they have to be like in order to make us look and feel better, then we're treading a dangerous path from the beginning.

Another example of when over-parenting can lead to real problems is a clinical phenomenon that I am noticing more and more – children with extreme problems with potty training because they have been pushed into potty training too early in order to get them into THE nursery school. Yes – children whose natural development in key areas of functioning is being accelerated because it suits our vanities and neuroses as parents. So we try to force early potty training or tutor our children within an inch of their life to ensure that they are the brightest and the best. We end up having children who are still pooing in their pants at five, hate reading and can't stand us. Nice work!

Always try to reflect on the long term and think about parenting logically: if I push my child this much now, and I accelerate development in one area, superficially or substantially, where is it going to give in another area? You can't have everything; it's about finding a balance.

I often ask parents very simply to relax – to take the pressure off themselves and their children. For some parents, even playing a game with their child turns into a task that they have to control. OK, they decide, this is the game we're going to play. No. Let your child choose the game. And then I watch parents saying, 'No, no, no, darling, not like that. No! No! No!' They forget to say, 'Well done! That's an interesting way of doing it. Oh, how funny!' – making a joke. It all suddenly becomes, 'No! My child doesn't have the correct pincer movement for this jigsaw!'

Or a child with an eating problem might have a mother or father who is obsessed about hygiene. It's OK that your child gets food everywhere – jelly on the floor, jelly in their hair, jelly on their cheek. It'll go in their mouth eventually and they'll love food and the process of eating. And you'll have a few brilliant shots to add to that series of photos to embarrass them with at their eighteenth birthday party.

Over-parenting, which is often done with a notion of accelerating one's child's development, can be best understood by the following little analogy:

Imagine a genetically modified tomato that has been grown at an accelerated rate, in a super-cyber greenhouse, using the most up-to-date and scientifically modified chemicals and compounds. What you will get is a very large, perfectly round, ripe-looking red tomato that looks as if it has been developed in the most perfect way. However, these tomatoes, when you bite into them – as we all know – taste of nothing.

And that is my point. If you over-parent and accelerate your child's development, you are likely to get a child who, superficially may look as if they are able to attain a higher level of achievement in many areas. But in getting to that point they will have had to compromise on so many other vital childhood experiences that they will be found lacking and wanting in other substantial areas of their lives, in terms of emotional and communication skills, for example. Gently nurture and encourage them to be the unique individual they are meant to be. Let *them* show *you* the way.

Questions to ask yourself:

Do you become anxious if your child is not developmentally ahead or up with others?

Are you investing more time in 'educational activities' than allowing them to just be?

Are you confusing ability with personality; attainment with contentment?

Tolerance

Really be prepared to tolerate the fact that there are some things you can't change. Children are not recipes, so the techniques won't always work. Sometimes they will cross the boundaries, but deep down they are superb human beings. And learn to live with the painful parts of your own life; this kind of tolerance is part of what makes successful living.

Parents will say, 'I will not tolerate my four-year-old saying, "I hate you, Mummy!"' It's just words; they don't know what hate is, and, if they do hate you for this moment, they'll get over it. Emotions come and go, they ebb and flow like the tides. And that's again why we have to go back and look at ourselves, because you're projecting onto your child something that has nothing to do with them.

We want our children to love us, and to feel loved by us. Love is the bedrock, an experience of feeling safe, feeling nurtured, feeling respected, feeling cared for, feeling all those things and more, but love is sometimes also tolerating the fact that you're not being liked so much. Being a parent and being a friend are two very different things. You want to be your children's friend all the time, but as their parent you can't expect that when you're teaching them some of life's tougher lessons. But you have to just get over that and go for it, and eventually help your children understand that that's the way things are. When you discipline your child, they won't like you for it, but it won't take away their love and ultimately will engender a sense of respect.

In many ways our children are our salvation, because they provide us with an opportunity to reflect on things. I worked with a woman who was very depressed, and had a little girl with big problems. This woman thought her daughter hated her, but I suggested that her daughter's behaviour was honestly showing how bad things were for Mum. Her actions were saying, 'Mummy, I'm worried. Mummy, things are bad.' We're teaching our children how to live life, while at the same time struggling to ive it ourselves. This is a chance to look at your life and the way you do things because you are teaching this little person how to be an emotionally rounded human being. And you might repeat things that were done to you that were problematic but have also resulted in you being who you are: a really great person.

I knew a couple where the husband had experienced a very difficult childhood. He was close to his parents but they separated when he was young, and his dad was quite aggressive. This couple had three children, a girl, then a boy, then another girl. He was absolutely fantastic with his first daughter, and responded to her extremely well. He then really wanted a son, but when their son did come along, he had a huge emotional response to the birth, and when he saw his son in his partner's arms, he felt a wave of intense envy. He fell apart as a parent and literally did not know what to do, not because he didn't love his son – he loved him more than anything in the world – and not because he was a bad parent, because he was a fantastic parent to the first child, who was a daughter. But that little boy's arrival just brought back so much of what he had experienced in his own childhood that he found it impossible to separate the two.

Now the three kids are much older, and he and his son have a fantastic relationship. This father was very courageous and did a lot of thinking and work on the intense emotions he was experiencing. He realized what was happening and was very open about it. I remember he just broke down in a session and cried, and said, 'I love this little boy but he makes me feel so sad. I don't know why.'

What does your child represent to you? What do they bring out in you? What is your child's behaviour saying about you? Is it saying, 'But, Mummy, sometimes you give me chocolate and sometimes you don't and Daddy always does. Mummy, if you say no, I know I can get Daddy to do it,' which is about looking at the way you parent as a couple and set limits? Or is their behaviour about a new baby in the house or you and your partner not getting on so well, or because you are so stressed about financial problems? What is the behaviour reflecting? Is this behaviour purely developmental or is it telling you that something isn't right somewhere? Could it be something that is very simply fixed, using behaviour techniques, or is it something more significant? That's what we need to try to find out.

And it's not that you have to then rush into therapy and heal the past, but that you have enough insight for you to catch yourself when you're about to go 'RAAAAHHHH' to something, take a deep breath and walk away, realizing, no, that's not about what's really happening. It's also about accepting that sometimes you can't do that at the time but afterwards you can learn from the experience and allow your child to see that as well, by offering a heartfelt apology with a clear explanation. Ultimately, it's all to do with being honest about yourself and accepting of yourself – you may have flaws (who doesn't) but those flaws don't have to stop you enjoying being a parent and can in fact enable you to be a more rounded and realistic parent.

Being a parent is the most incredible privilege and can be the most enormous pleasure – if you allow it to be. It's about being honest and about having courage, and it's about also recognizing that you're in a relationship with someone who makes you feel the very best emotions in the world but also the worst: out of control, angry, sad, desperate, hopeless and even helpless.

Remember, they're only small. They haven't been here very long; they don't understand the rules of the game yet. That's what we're here to do – teach them.

I felt hesitant about putting this Q & A section in because it might seem that we are back in the land of child behaviour = problem ➜ solution; quick questions about children leading to easy answers. However, I wanted to include it because it gives us the opportunity to pull all our thinking together with some real examples of parental dilemmas that I heard amongst the groups of parents I spoke to when writing *Your Child ... Your Way*.

My hope is that in reading this section you are now at a stage where you won't be searching desperately for the example that fits your child and then feel disappointed when you don't, but that you read the question and then maybe before reading my response work out what advice you would give. In essence, the advice needs to reflect the core aspects of being a positive parent, which are: feeling confident in yourself even when the situation is extremely challenging; looking at your child's behaviour and asking yourself what it means and what could be triggering it; thinking about your responses and then trying to bring clarity, consistency and a sense of calm to the response.

Ultimately, the underlying principle comes from the notion that what we think affects what we feel and therefore impacts significantly on how we behave. Therefore, memorizing every technique in part Part Two of this book will have no impact on how successful you and your child are at resolving the difficulties you both face if you have no fundamentally positive beliefs in yourself as a parent (despite how you might be feeling) and in your child (despite how they might be behaving). Any anxious, negative beliefs will lead to panic as you read the examples and think, 'Oh no! That's not how I would do it – I'll have to go back and relearn all the techniques!' or, 'My child doesn't behave exactly in that way so how can I use the advice given here?'

You need to challenge these beliefs immediately and reflect on what it is about you that has shifted positively in the reading of this book – how have you changed in your perceptions and actions? So if you find yourself disagreeing with my advice – that's fine, providing that your thoughts fit well with the way you perceive yourself and your child.

Remember – the notion of expert can become dangerous and overblown when it begins to erode the confidence of others who are living the issues about which the expertise is given. I am a clinical psychologist giving clinical advice – I am not the expert on your child, your family, your life: you are.

So let us all read on feeling confident that in each of us there are the skills, the understanding and most importantly the confidence to think about difficult situations and see positive ways forward.

Our four-year-old daughter has become very scared to be alone, she won't leave my side during the day and if we try to go into another room she cries. Her fear seems very real and we just don't know what to do for the best.

Anxiety disorders are one of the primary mental-health problems affecting children and adolescents today. Most children, when asked, are able to report having several fears at any given age and research has shown that 90% of children between the ages of two and fourteen have at least one specific fear that is often natural and arises at specific times in their development, tending to disappear naturally with time as the child grows older. Examples of common fears at specific ages are:

Infants/toddlers (0–2 years): loud noises, strangers, separation from parents, large objects.
Preschoolers (3–6 years): imaginary figures (e.g., ghosts, monsters, aliens), the dark, noises, sleeping alone, wild weather.
School-aged children/adolescents (7–16 years): more realistic fears (e.g., physical injury, health, school performance, death, thunderstorms).

The most common fears to affect children are: generalized anxiety disorder, panic disorder, separation anxiety disorder and specific phobias.

Generalized anxiety disorder (GAD) is characterized by excessive worrying about a variety of issues and events (past, present and future) – most of the time in a manner that cannot be controlled and that interferes with functioning.

Panic disorder is characterized by recurring panic attacks that are inappropriately linked to physical or psychological harm. They take the form of intense fear with physical symptoms including increased heart rate and chest pain, choking and difficulty breathing, sweating and trembling, hot or cold flushes, dizziness, numbness or tingling in the limbs and a number of fearful thoughts, including fear of dying or going mad. These attacks then lead to the avoidance of places and engaging in activities.

Separation anxiety disorder refers typically to younger children who are distressed and extremely anxious about separating from major attachment figures (e.g., parents, grandparents, older siblings) or from home, resulting in anxiety. Nightmares and somatic complaints are common, inducing trembling, headaches, nausea, vomiting, stomach pain and sweating.

Children may experience specific phobias, which are intense, irrational fears and associated with anxiety and distress about certain things or situations (e.g., dogs, bees, injections, the dark, escalators, tunnels, flying, etc.). Children may then avoid the feared object and this can lead to significant disruption to social, emotional and psychological functioning.

Cognitive-behavioural therapy is the treatment for an anxiety disorder and focuses on teaching children anxiety management skills: to recognize anxious feelings regarding their thoughts and to identify their associated physical reactions and the impact on their behaviour. They are taught to identify their thoughts in anxiety-provoking situations, and are taught coping strategies such as relaxation and thought control. Children are guided in developing a list of situations that are challenging for them, and then taught to implement their coping skills while gradually facing each of these situations (this is called systematic desensitization). Parents are often taught new ways to interact with their children so that the child's fears are not inadvertently reinforced. Parents are also taught ways to give children ample praise and positive reinforcement for brave behaviour.

Given the wide range of tasks children must accomplish throughout their childhood, it is imperative to ensure that their level of anxiety does not begin to interfere with their ability to function. If it does, it is important that they begin to learn some skills for coping more efficiently with their anxious feelings or we are not giving them the most vital coping strategies for life. A great book to read is *Overcoming Your Child's Fears and Worries* by Cathy Cresswell and Lucy Willetts.

My child is very clingy and I'm dreading when she starts nursery. What do I do?

Separation anxiety is a very normal part of development and toddler behaviour. When a child reaches about eight months they might begin to show fear of separation and also of strangers – a child who would be left happily with a friend while you went out to make a cup of tea suddenly screams blue murder and can only be consoled by you. Toddlers tend to go through a phase of neophobia, which can be attached to any new kind of experience, whether meeting new people or trying new foods or wearing new kinds of clothes. They can become very anxious and unwilling to have any new experience.

The experience of separation anxiety is also symbolic of the process of individuation that a toddler goes through. This is an inner separation between their mother or their primary care giver and themselves, and an understanding or an emerging awareness that they are an individual with their own thoughts and beliefs and behaviours that can have an impact on others.

All children will show some degree of separation anxiety at particular transitional points in their development, starting nursery for example, and this should be seen as healthy and normal. Some children seemingly breeze through the experience and are raring to go, running into nursery, whereas others will hold on to your leg with a strength you never knew they had, or might be extremely tearful and unwilling to leave your side.

If you have a child who seems to have some clingy behaviours and you have concerns about upcoming separation anxieties, it is always useful to expose your child to as many different social experiences as possible with yourself present, and also to encourage them gently to go off and play, and spend as much time as they can away from you, even if you are in the environment. Organized play dates with friends or spending a few hours with a grandparent or someone you and they trust will help them get used to the process of separation before the major separational milestone when they start nursery.

The last important thing to say is that the way your child will deal with their separation anxiety is very much tied to the way you respond. The more positive and calm you can be when your child is showing a huge anxiety response, and the more you can trust the staff at the nursery to take your child and get them engaged in this new environment, the better for your child. So only start sobbing (I know I did) when you are out of their sight and can do so safely without causing them more anxiety and fear.

How can I help my child who is extremely shy?

Shyness usually occurs around six months of age but will diminish over time as a child begins to be more socially adept. However, some children can go on to develop acute shyness in social situations and will not wish to be left by their parent or leave them to join a group. Often I have found that the parents themselves may be quite reserved and so for them to try and push their little one off to join others is painful. Clearly children need to develop social skills and need to be able to leave us in order to thrive and have a variety of developmental experiences. But every child is unique and should be respected for their personality and temperament. As a parent, remember you are their role model and so try to model interaction skills. Also use the gradual withdrawal method suggested in the sleep section and take your child to a social setting and then gradually move further away from them as they get involved in play while you remain in their vision.

My child says they are afraid of the dark. How can I tell the difference between real fear and behaviour to avoid going to bed?

Children who experience fear will show the same physiological signs that we as adults experience when we are stressed or fearful: they may become pale, start to sweat, shake or hyperventilate; they may want to go to the toilet a lot, say they feel sick or become tearful and agitated.

If you have a child who is afraid of the dark, very gently enable them to feel they have some mastery and control of the dark by using a number of creative parenting skills. A small night light is useful, although it is important to say do not leave an overhead light on because that will impact on the quality of the sleep that your child is getting, which would have a detrimental effect on their development.

For older children, you can leave different little zappers by the bed that they may use if they feel afraid, little water pistols or whatever, anything that, cognitively, they can hang their fear on and begin to feel that they have more mastery of the dark.

If you find that a child's fear of the dark is disrupting their ability to go to sleep at night, then use the gradual withdrawal method – slowly separate yourself over a number of days from the child by sitting further and further away from them as they fall asleep. This enables them to build their confidence and to recognize that the dark is not to be afraid of, that it is a time when they can comfortably and safely fall asleep.

The dark is scary, it is something that we need to feel comfortable in and master. A lot of children have so many noises and sounds and lights on when they go to sleep that they don't ever learn to be comfortable with a dark environment, and the fear can then build over time. A common trigger for problems is when a sibling comes along and they are then expected to be on their own in their bed.

There is also a very rare condition called night-vision blindness, which is when you can't even make out shapes in the dark and your vision becomes pitted, as though there are big holes in front of you. It is extremely rare but does explain some children's fear of the dark.

My child is very attached to their blanket and takes it everywhere. Does this mean they are anxious and neurotic?

Some children do carry a blanket and many years ago this was seen as being illustrative of an anxious and neurotic personality. However, thinking has changed and it is now seen as being entirely appropriate for a child to have what is called a transitional object, such as a blanket, a teddy, or any other object that they can carry that comforts them. The view is that this object is a transition between being attached to the parent and separating from them. Your child associates their blanket with home, with being safe and comfortable, and is something they can then take with them in a new environment and have when you aren't with them. These objects symbolize what children attach to the relationship with their primary carer, and therefore it enables them to make that transition into a new environment, plus any separation, with greater ease. If your child has a transitional object, then that is fine; they will eventually leave it behind as they get older and more confident about being in different social situations without you.

My daughter, who is nearly three, has an imaginary friend who always sits next to her and is blamed when anything gets knocked over or something more naughty has occurred. Is this normal or should I worry?

For some children this is normal and therefore I wouldn't worry. I had an imaginary friend and would also insist that a place at the table be laid for them – I'm not sure if that reassures you or not! One way of managing the issue of the friend being blamed for mishaps would be to assertively deal with your child for whatever behaviour has occurred and so let them know that you are aware of their responsibility in the situation and also think up some positive things that the friend could be responsible for.

I'm worried about giving my child a dummy but sometimes I think it would help my sanity! What do you think?

Children shouldn't really need to have dummies at all, but some babies do cry a lot, and so dummies are useful. Sometimes I work with mothers whose babies just cry and cry and they can get very depressed and so a dummy helps.

Dummies do pacify, but they also push down on the tongue so these muscles of the mouth are delayed in their development. This can often lead to a delay in speech development in terms of articulation, which can in turn lead to a child's frustration that they can't communicate their emotions. If you keep pacifying the tantrums with a dummy, you're compounding the problem, plus your child won't learn how to control their temper if it is just being 'plugged' all the time.

So, dummies can be helpful in the short term, but they really don't help in the long term. If you can get rid of them, cold turkey it and put up with the ensuing tantrums, it will be worth it. Many parents find that encouraging their child to literally throw away their own dummies can be an effective way to get rid of them. Another good idea is to be creative and think of a great story to attach to letting go of the dummies – for example using the classic tooth-fairy story but this time with dummies!

My son is one year old and has a fear of pushchairs, shopping trolleys and baby walkers. As soon as I even lift him near to his pushchair (and we have tried different ones) he screams, cries real tears and becomes completely traumatized.

I think we live in a society overrun with people like me who work within an industry that could be seen to have created its own business. Certainly, I have parents coming to me for advice on 'problems' with their children that are born out of their own insecurities as parents and focus on anything that may be damaging to their child. Children were once expected to 'get on with it' – if they cried but they were clearly in no danger and were safe and being loved, crying was tolerated as part of the process. Your question highlights to me an inability to manage your own parental anxiety, and so you project it onto your child, i.e., they cry in the buggy, you lift them out and cuddle them. You are inadvertently showing them there is something to be afraid of. In so doing, because you have been unable to just strap your child in and leave them to cry because they are having a tantrum, I suspect you have created this problem by pairing your anxiety response towards your crying child when they are in the buggy with taking them away from the buggy, and eventually putting the buggy away. Hence, in your son's mind there is definitely now something to be afraid of.

  The bottom line is this: if your child is fearful of a situation that is entirely safe, then they must be helped to see this and continually put into that situation calmly and assertively even if they are screaming their little heads off at the beginning. Eventually they will learn that there is nothing to be afraid of. Fears and phobias are treated either by systematic desensitization: gradual exposure to the feared object, so this would mean trips out in the buggy for increasing lengths of time; or flooding, which would mean strapping him in, going for a long walk, letting him scream and just getting on with it.

My five-year-old daughter is extremely mature for her age in terms of her verbal reasoning and comprehension. She recently asked me about babies and said, 'How does the seed get in your tummy and where does the baby come out?' What do I say?

There are so many parents who share your concerns and are preoccupied with how to discuss sex with their children. I think it is imperative that we all take a deep breath, relax and recognize that when our child asks we must be prepared to answer honestly, without embarrassment, in a way that they will understand. For a child to know about sex does not equal a loss of innocence, just age-appropriate curiosity about where babies come from in the same way they will be curious about so many other interesting aspects of the world that is unfolding before them. She has a curiosity that does not relate to sexual intercourse and the act of love making as we adults construe sex, but to the mechanics of her body and how on earth babies can come from inside anyone's body and, by the way, how did it get in there in the first place? She wonders this in the same way that we might ponder over how a ship got into a bottle. However, as soon as we put our adult interpretation on things, we get anxious and embarrassed, our children sense there is something more to this getting-a-baby-into-the-tummy lark than they are being told and, worst-case scenario, they see this whole baby business as something that is secretive, shameful and not to be talked about.

Teaching your children about sex demands a gentle, continuous flow of information that should begin as early as possible. This means not avoiding questions and telling the truth at a level that can be processed. I also believe strongly that this means teaching children the anatomically correct words for their genitals: little girls have a vagina, they have labia and vulva and little boys have a penis and testicles. Why on earth do we have our children call their genitals by ridiculous euphemisms when we are quite comfortable for them to call their ear an ear and their toe a toe? Does the fact that a little girl knows her vagina mean she is somehow sexually too aware or using a 'dirty' word? No, it means she knows about her body.

The less you say, the more she'll ask. Tailor the information to her level of understanding and while she won't be able to get her head around intercourse she will understand that she happened when mummy's egg and daddy's sperm met and joined together – how you describe that I'll leave to you, but there are many books that can help you, such as *Mummy Laid an Egg!* by Babette Cole, which is excellent and fun. I have Claire Rayner's *The Body Book*, which is quite old but, like the author herself, is clear, down-to-earth and informative in a no-nonsense, non-threatening way.

My ten-month-old daughter cries constantly unless I'm holding her. I have tried leaving her to cry but she will cry for over an hour if I leave her.

There are babies who cry more than most and this can cause a huge amount of stress and distress to the rest of the members of the family. A baby's cry is an effective method of communication given their absolute helplessness and dependency on us – it alerts us immediately and causes us to stop all other activity until we can understand what our baby needs and how we can accommodate it. A baby's cry is so powerful that it can cause an immediate 'let-down reflex' in the breastfeeding mother –

unconsciously responding to the possibility that the cry comes from a need to feed. When my children were babies, I can remember how the cries of my friend's babies would engender a want to pick up their infant but in a relaxed and non-urgent way; if it was my child, however, I could feel every muscle tense as I rushed to them, pushing all others out of my path! This is all natural but if you have a baby who cries more often than not and is difficult to soothe, it can be extremely difficult and stressful, causing us to think less logically and more emotionally.

I suggest that you respond to their crying by working your way through a checklist of possibilities and if by the end none have helped then at least you can reassure yourself that you have done everything you can.

- **Are they hungry or thirsty?** Feed them; give them a drink.
- **Are they fighting the breast?** Speak to a breastfeeding counsellor.
- **Are they uncomfortable?** Move them, check their temperature, unwrap them or wrap them snugly, change their nappy.
- **Do they need to be held?** Holding a young baby is very important in terms of the developing attachment and bond you have with them, so don't be afraid to hold or rock and at times use the sling so that they can be near you and you can get on and do things.
- **Are they overstimulated?** They want to sleep but can't because of light, noise, activity – take them somewhere calm.
- **Are they under-stimulated?** Some babies are stopped from crying by singing or the rhythmic noise of the washing machine or vacuum cleaner – the noises they were used to in their uterine environment before birth.
- **Are they ill?** An ill child usually cries in a more urgent way but, if you have concerns, trust your instincts and call your GP, health visitor or NHS Direct.
- **Are they just cranky and fretful?** Why shouldn't they be – it's a big new world for them. Try baby massage or tummy rubbing for a baby with colic. Some parents have found cranial osteopathy (the laying on of hands to restore a necessary balance to the structures of the

skeleton) very helpful for their fretful baby: the notion being that their crying is reduced with the gentle treatment of an uncomfortable head pressure following the birth.

Do they want to suck? This is where dummies can help if the crying has gone on for so long that you are beginning to lose it!

There may be times when nothing works and you then have to focus on dealing with your own response to the crying. If your baby is clearly fed, changed and safe, walk out of the room for short periods to get away from the noise. Play some music, call a friend – switch your focus for just a short time so that you can lower your stress when you respond to your child's cries.

I am unsure whether my child is a fussy eater or has certain food phobias.

A phobia is an irrational and exaggerated response to a stimulus that does not require or deserve that response, so for example a child becoming completely hysterical when they are presented with a plate of broccoli. Broccoli is clearly a neutral and unthreatening object, but for that child – because of the level of anxiety that they have about any kind of new food experience – they will then develop an anxiety reaction which will cause them to show phobic behaviour. This can manifest itself in a number of ways, such as not being able to pick up the food, not being able to touch the food, not being able to tolerate having the food anywhere near them and ultimately just wanting to avoid the food at all costs.

A fussy eater is often a child who is manipulating a parent by their behaviour. The problem is often compounded because the parent will offer them many different types of foods in order to get the child to eat.

A phobic child will show a genuinely acute anxiety reaction to a new food that is presented, and again this reaction should not be confused with a tantrum, which is fuelled by anger and rage at not getting their own way. An anxiety reaction has much more the sense of a child being truly out of their depth and unable to cope with what it is that they are being faced with.

As with any phobia, the way of managing it is called systematic desensitization, which means very slowly and gently presenting the child with whatever it is that they are phobic about. As discussed on page 118, research has shown that a child needs to be presented with a new food that they have never experienced before between fifteen and twenty times before they will even consent to pick it up, so just put a small bit of the food on the plate, say nothing and leave it, and slowly build up exposure until your child is able to just prod it with their finger, eventually lick it, and so on and so on.

The problem with food phobias is that because, for parents, feeding is such a primal role, parents will become extremely anxious about their child's behaviour. The anxiety is projected back onto the child, who will then see that there is something truly to fear. And so the situation will compound itself. I know it's easy to say, but be calm. Feed your child what you know they are comfortable with, don't panic about the nutritional content, and understand that only very slowly and calmly, with a number of presentations and creative ways of getting your child to feel comfortable with new food, will they pick it up and, eventually, taste it.

How important are the links between diet and behaviour?

There is no doubt that there is a link between diet and behaviour, not only in terms of the quality of the food ingested but quantity of food ingested. Although I am not a dietician, it seems very clear that a child must be given a healthy and nutritionally balanced diet hat enables them to develop and grow in the best way possible. Some children do show food intolerances and this can be displayed via their behaviour – having problems sleeping, for example, or becoming prone to tantrums – and it can be very useful to test for allergies. However, as a note of caution, many behaviour problems with food and eating come from a parental overanxiety and over-preoccupation with their child's diet, and so in attempting to give their child a healthy and nutritionally balanced diet their own neurosis becomes so profound that the child associates food with anxiety and therefore becomes very stressed about eating.

My child will only fall asleep playing with my hair, which is becoming a problem. What should I do?

Children will commonly show different ways of comforting themselves when they are relaxing and/or going to sleep. Silking is a term that refers to a child who will stroke the edge of a blanket or a soft piece of material for comfort. The tactile stimulation is seen as being self-soothing and for some children becomes an association for sleep, so that they are then only able to fall asleep if they have that little bit of blanket or whatever it is that they need to touch before they go to sleep.

   If you have a child whose comfort habit or relaxing/sleep association is attached to you in some way, then this is a problem because as your child becomes more dependent on, in this case, your hair as a comforting device that they need to twiddle, hold, wrap round their fingers in order to be able to go to sleep, so your hair, therefore you, will need to be with them whenever your child wakes in the night and they need to go back to sleep.

   You need to wean your child off your hair and give them a different kind of comforter with which to associate sleep until they are old enough to learn to fall asleep without it.

My daughter has started stammering when she speaks. Should I get her assessed?

Some children go through a period of stammering as they develop their language and communication skills. This is often because, cognitively, they are moving a lot faster in terms of their thoughts and what they *want* to say than the motor ability to articulate those words, so children will stammer because they are tripping themselves up trying to speak faster than they can.

If this is something that has been going on for some time and you see it most of the time when she communicates, then it is worth talking to your health visitor or your GP about a referral to see a speech and language therapist. However, if this is around an event that is just occurring at a specific point in her development and doesn't happen every time she communicates, it is possibly just a transient feature of her speech and language development that she will soon grow out of.

My toddler has been diagnosed with ADHD. Is any of your parenting advice relevant to the management of this?

ADHD stands for Attention Deficit Hyperactivity Disorder and you may also have had a diagnosis of ADD which means Attention Deficit Disorder. Children with these difficulties often show a range of behaviours linked with an inability to attend to any task for a specific period of time, problems with concentration, difficulties in settling and sitting still, and needing constant external stimulation. For children who have this clinical diagnosis, there are pharmacological treatment approaches that have been found to be very helpful in some cases.

As far as managing a child with ADHD or ADD goes, that child is still an individual with their own individual wants and needs, and, emotionally, should be parented in the same way as any other child. It is important to see that they are a child with a condition rather than just a condition in itself. Children with ADHD respond as well to order and routine and structure as any child. It helps them feel safe and contained. Also, for a child with ADHD it is very important that they have an understanding of the boundaries round their behaviour and the consequences of unacceptable behaviour. Clear messages are essential. Treat your child with ADHD as you would any other child – because that is what they are – with a combination of understanding, empathy, patience, firmness, authority, love and respect.

Our son has been labelled as destructive in his nursery class and is clearly struggling to cope. His behaviour is becoming increasingly difficult for his teacher. How can we work together to support him?

It is very important, indeed it is the central theme of the book, to understand that any individual child's behaviour is a function and a feature of where they are, who they are with and what else is going on in the context and the environment in which they are developing. Children who are extremely disruptive in classroom settings or nursery settings may be manifesting via their behaviour underlying difficulties that they have socially, or in their communication skills or learning. There is ample evidence that children who have specific learning difficulties will often be first labelled as 'difficult' children because that behaviour develops as a way of compensating for the underlying and extreme challenges that they may have in a learning environment.

Having an ability to think broadly about a child's behaviour does not mean that one is condoning their behaviour, nor making excuses for it, but is a way of thinking about them in a way that acknowledges that their behaviour is a function of external as well as internal factors. These factors need to be considered before the child is labelled and their behaviour dismissed out of hand. To be able to have a conversation with a teacher who has this broad breadth of focus would be very helpful for you all at this time.

My child seems to have an erratic attention span and poor concentration. What could that mean?

Toddlers have a huge series of developmental milestones to get through in a relatively short space of time. There are enormous cognitive thinking changes going on as well as physiological growth, and huge learning and communication challenges, both in terms of speech development and the much bigger challenge that comes with a developing understanding of themselves and who they are in terms of the world and the people they function among.

In order to achieve these various developmental milestones and tasks, children will not display a linear way of learning and developing but, rather, will have developmental spurts in some areas while appearing to stall in others. For example, a child might seem to be developing physically, yet seems unable to progress their speech and language skills for a certain period of time, so the developmental demands on a child can show themselves in erratic abilities to attend and to concentrate. These are often at times when a child has literally reached developmental overload and just needs to be left to assimilate the information that they have absorbed.

It's important to make sure your child has a very good sleep pattern and a balanced diet with regular mealtimes to aid healthy development. When they enter preschool, then school, and you find this erratic attention span and poor concentration continues, it may then be time to have a more specific look at your child's learning abilities. Right now, though, you need to be calm, relaxed and supportive of your child and allow them to learn at their own pace, which includes their own attention span and their own concentration levels, rather than a pace that you feel is right.

My child has physical disabilities and often gets frustrated when playing and will sometimes end up hitting his friends. I find it difficult to discipline this behaviour because I feel guilty.

This is a very understandable and difficult situation. You can see that your child's behaviour is linked to their disability and associated frustration, and that is bound to bring up all sorts of feelings in you as their parent, including, I suspect, much guilt and sadness that your child finds themselves in this situation. You may even be blaming yourself on some level for the fact that your child has physical disabilities. The key issue here is to see your child for who they are and celebrate your child for who they are. Also, their physical disabilities are a part of who they are, and that cannot be changed. Therefore, you would be doing your child no favours if you did not parent them in a way that allowed them to learn the key social skills necessary for them to go on to develop positive healthy relationships and friendships with other people.

While entirely understandable, making allowances for your child's frustrations because of your own guilt and sensitivity to them could have a greater impact on them in the long term because you are denying them an important part of their learning a human being – which is that we do not hit when we feel frustrate we have to find other ways of dealing with our frustration. For a child for whom frustration may be a feature of their life, both in childhood and in adulthood, this is actually a very important lesso and one I would suggest you ensure you feel confident in teaching firmly, and with kindness and compassion.

My stepdaughter is on the autistic spectrum and at times her behaviour can be very challenging and aggressive. What are the most suitable ways of responding to that behaviour?

Children who have a diagnosis on the autistic spectrum disorder have a number of behaviours linked to this diagnosis that can be a challenging for those who live with them as for the child themselve For many children with such a diagnosis there are flash points in communication and relationships that can cause them to feel unsettled, unhappy and threatened, which sets off a chain of behaviour that can become both aggressive and difficult to manag

As with any child who has any kind of difficulties related to a physical, emotional or mental diagnosis it is important to recogniz them as a child first and their diagnosis second. Any child who is parented according to a label that they have been given will have a significantly greater number of problems than a child who is parented as an individual child. An autistic child raised as an autistic child would then have those associated aspects to who the are, in this case autism. It is very important for children with any kind of autistic spectrum difficulties to be shown clearly, consistently, firmly and gently that their aggressive behaviour is unacceptable. The earlier this can be done, the easier it is in the long run because the child's behaviour can be shaped.

Is it better to stay together for the sake of the children?

There is a good deal of research to indicate that children who are raised in atmospheres marked by hostility and aggression will go on to develop behavioural and emotional difficulties. It is not appropriate to stay together for the sake of the children unless the attempt is marked by work done by both parents to address their emotional issues, so that the staying together also heralds the dawn of a more healthy and better relationship.

Staying together in itself can be incredibly destructive as children then become responsible to some degree for both parents remaining in a relationship that is causing unhappiness for the whole family. If a relationship is understood to be beyond any kind of long-term improvement so that separation really is the only option, then the separation should be done responsibly and amicably. It is critical that the children are spared any sense of having any kind of role in that separation and that none of the hostility associated with the separation is played out through those children.

Children who live with parents who are separated and happier in themselves as individuals, and who can continue to co-parent those children in a way that is nurturing and loving because the children's interests are at the heart of everything, do better than those who are growing up in a family with atmospheres of tension and hostility because parents had stayed together for their sake.

It is very important when couples separate that they have some support to really think about the impact of their separation on their children and how any of the tension or hostility associated to the separation can be played out through the children. Family mediation centres can be very useful to enable separating or separated parents to find a common and agreed parenting style.

Bringing up my children alone, I struggle to be both mum and dad. How can I achieve this?

You can't. If you are mum, you are mum and if you are dad, you are dad, but you can't be both. It's important that your children have a range of close relationships where they can have role models of the opposite gender, but it's equally important that your children understand that they are a product of a one-parent family, and that one parent is either mum or dad.

What is interesting about this question is that it implies that there is a gender split in terms of parenting. Both mothers and fathers should hold the same parental qualities, which are to be loving, caring, nurturing, calm, kind, patient, authoritative and strict as and when necessary. But often what is missing in a family with a sole parent are the gender attributes that come with the role modelling of certain gender behaviours. For daughters brought up by a father, for example, they may need other close relationships with older women who can enable them to think about their own gender development.

The fundamental aspects of parenting cut across both genders however, and no parent should ever feel that they have to try and embody mum *and* dad. Be who you are and be comfortable with that because it's only when we feel comfortable with who we are that we can parent the most effectively.

?

re my children losing out being brought up in a single-
arent home?

hildren have the best upbringing from parents who are happy,
ttled and confident in themselves both as individuals and as
arents. If, as a single parent, you see this as a handicap to your
nildren, then it will be because the perception you bring to your
arenting which comes from your perception of yourself will have
huge impact on your children. Your children are being brought
p by *you*, and this is something to be celebrated because as their
arent you are the one who knows most instinctively what is best
r them in terms of their ongoing development through their
nildhood and into their adulthood.

Bringing a positive feel to your parenting ability will have a
uge impact on your children. If you come at your parenting with
ne belief that your children are losing out, then this will reflect in
our parenting and have a detrimental impact on your children.

Single parenting can be very draining when you've got this
ttle one who needs constant care, but there's also a part of you
at just needs to be alone and have a bit of space. When you're
aving to do all of that on your own, it is much more difficult.
nd as a single parent your child may want to cuddle you more
ecause sometimes children can be very receptive emotionally,
r they can see how tired you are. There's a lot to be said for being
uite creative in parenting although, of course, that's easier said
nan done when you're feeling exhausted. But you could say,
)K, let's have a two-minute cuddle and then let's run into the
tchen, and let's draw a monster!' And then he draws a monster
n his own while you get a chance to get on with things, and
ou've made it into a game – if you can find the energy to do that.

?

Is there any such thing as middle-child syndrome?

Middle-child syndrome exists because it's a label that has been attributed to middle children for as long as anyone can remember. Certainly birth order does have an impact on the development of personality but much of this comes with expectation and by what we perceive they will have to deal with either as the first born, the middle, or the third and so on.

It is important to be sensitive to the birth order of all children in a family: the first who may have to grow up quickly when subsequent siblings come along, the youngest who may be held back and babied because they are known to be the last baby of that family, the child in the middle who maybe never feels they have a specific role. For each of these children their birth order can bring both challenges and also privileges and it is important to be aware of that when you are considering their behaviour and any difficulties that you may have with them.

My toddler is upset about the birth of her baby sister. How can I handle this?

The birth of a new child will often cause an emotional response from a sibling who has, up until that point, been the only child and the focus of all the love and attention of all parents, grandparents and other family members. It also heralds a shift in the perception you have as parents who suddenly have a new baby and see your toddler as inhabiting a different role in the family. All these shifts are going to have an impact on everyone concerned, but the older sibling will be the one who will likely how these shifts more obviously in terms of their behaviour, which will often become regressed as they struggle to cope with the birth of a new sibling.

So, for example, toilet-trained children may start to wet themselves, or children previously in a good sleep pattern may start to not sleep well. They are showing via their behaviour the emotional response they have to a sibling. After you have given your child some space and some understanding in terms of the transitional adjustment reaction they are having to the birth of their sibling, it is important to be very clear with them around their behaviour and to not allow any aggressive behaviour to be directed towards the baby.

You can do this creatively by setting up lots of play opportunities for your toddler with your baby and also one just with you when the baby is asleep. But if things get out of hand, remember to use very clear behavioural strategies such as asking once nicely, once firmly and then setting up a consequence so that the child can understand clearly the reason this has happened is because they were aggressive to their baby brother or sister and that must not happen any more.

Make sure you praise every positive interaction. This is an effective way of shaping a child's behaviour but also reminds you to really praise his loveliness. Set up special playtimes with her and the baby with you observing her play with her and giving positive running commentary of all she does – trying not to correct her or become overly anxious if things get a little vigorous. At those times just gently remind her to 'be soft' and model gentle ways of playing for her. Also make sure you make plenty of alone time with her so she still has special time with Mummy that isn't intruded on by little sister. Finally, please know that this is a phase, it's a normal reaction and it does not mean your child has any nasty personality streak – she's just cross with you for having another baby. She'll get over it!

?

Our two children are both at school now, and have been at war with each other ever since the youngest came along. How can we ease the constant tension this creates?

If your children are at war with each other, then have a chat with your partner, or with a friend if you are single parenting, and think about what's going on and how stressful it is for everybody. Then cook a meal one night, sit down with your children and spell out your thoughts to them along the lines of 'this is what we both think, this is what is happening and this is what we don't like'. With older children you can say they've each got five minutes or two minutes or however long you can stand to say what they don't like about each other's behaviour. Write it all down and then let them know this is all about respect, and how you can bring more respect into your family relationships.

Now write a contract with your kids. For example, your daughter might say I don't want him to come into my room without knocking first. So that's one thing everyone agrees on for the contract. Or if your children can't be in a room together without arguing, then they are both to leave and go to their rooms. And you might find your children give you some useful feedback too. The important thing is for everyone to agree and sign the contract.

To enforce the contract you might need to impose a Response Cost. So if your children play on their computers for half an hour in the evening, you could then break that down into five- or ten-minute segments. And every time they break a rule in the contract, or after you've asked them twice and they're still not doing what you've asked them, you just put a cross through a segment, and say they've lost ten minutes. Or you could use three strikes and you're out on their weekly pocket money. The key

essage that your children will learn is that their behaviour is
oing to have an impact on their fun. And they may well have got
to a habit of yelling at each other, which you can help to break
y all sitting down calmly to discuss the contract.

?

**low can my partner and I prepare for the bringing
ogether of our two sets of children (seven in total)
when we all start living together?**

lended families are where two families come together and
ring a number of children with them – the classic fictional
xample being the Brady Bunch.

It is very important when two partners get together that the
hildren have as much preparation for this as possible. Don't
ush to move your two families together, and ensure the process
 facilitated by a number of meetings and opportunities for your
hildren to start to build relationships between them and an
nderstanding of this new way of living for the whole family.

Blended families often run into problems where there is a
udden collision of the two families with very little preparation
nd the parents having some expectation because of their love
or each other that the children will automatically follow suit.
This can often not be the case as children can become jealous,
ary and understandably uncomfortable with the new living
tuation and the new siblings that they have had forced upon
nem. As with any kind of major change in a child's life, any kind
f transition, it is vital that parents communicate openly, prepare
heir children fully and that children also feel they have the
pportunity to speak about how they feel and whether they have
ny fears about the new situation. In this way you can all look
fter each other and acknowledge that everybody has emotional
eeds in this new family set up.

It is difficult when families come together, because why should everybody automatically like each other just because the two people who are coming together have fallen in love? I have often experienced blended families where the two parents have someho looked for their relationship to be validated via their children's behaviour, in other words that their children are all happy and lov each other, and everyone can march on together into the sunset with joy and goodwill. In reality, life isn't like that and there can be many different feelings that need to be taken into account.

Both adults in the partnership should set up some very clear rules with each other for how they will parent, and also what the rules, expectations and boundaries round behaviour in the family are. This process is helped when children feel included and their needs are understood. However, with younger children actions speak louder than words and if there is any display of hostility or aggression, then this should be dealt with appropriately.

At the end of the day, love comes out of respect and respect comes out of an understanding of other people's needs. The more open a family can be about this and the more honest everyone can be about how they feel, combined with clarity of expectations around behaviour, the sooner children will find a way to form a relationship with each other.

My wife and I have split up and we have a three-year-old son. I have a new partner and will soon be moving away to live with her – how should I tell my son and introduce him to her?

The key is to be honest. Even very young children can pick up on feelings and atmospheres and have a rather accurate sense that something is going on. Unless there is an honest communication (but one that is appropriate for their age and spares them facts tha

ey would not be able to understand) many children begin to
ame themselves or see themselves as responsible for the tension.

If possible, I would try and plan with your ex-partner how you
an discuss the reality of the separation with your son. Even better,
y and do it together although this may be hard while feelings
e so raw.

It is important that you introduce him to your new partner so
at he feels part of your life and also that your new partner has a
ance to develop a relationship with him; again it would be best
this could be done with your ex-partner's blessing but that may
e hard. When you talk to your son you could do it while engaging
another activity because to sit him down and attempt a formal
xplanation may be very difficult and frightening for him. Often
is useful to set up a drawing session. You could try to steer the
ctivity so that you and he draw his family, and you can show him
at Mummy and Daddy are not next to each other any more and
ere is a new person next to Daddy. But Mummy and Daddy still
ve him in the middle of them because they love him very much
d will also always, together, want the best for him and look after
m jointly, although apart. This is hard to convey to a young child
words but can be explained via drawing and during play. Again,
you can help your ex-partner feel part of this explanation or at
ast ask for her thoughts on what would be the right way to say
, it might also be quite healing for the two of you.

Children are children but they are not stupid. Without the
phistication and complexities of the social and communication
ills that we as adults have that often cause us problems in
lationships, they have a simple, straightforward and often
ry clear perception of what is going on around them. In my
xperience, children of maturely separated couples fare better
an those who live with two parents locked in disharmony, but
urge you to make sure that any fallout from the break-up of your
lationship with his mother does not tip into him, and that you
oth, as adults, try and work together to ensure he is given a clear
d honest explanation of how his family now works.

As a working parent I don't want to come home and discipline my child but they can behave very badly. Because I see them so little, will I damage our relationship by being a disciplinarian?

Many working parents feel uneasy about disciplining their children when they get home because they feel so guilty about not having seen them all day. However, this can then lead into a spiral of out-of-control behaviour and overexcited kids who can't sleep or settle. This might lead to parental arguments and so evenings become tense and fraught. Who is happy then? In order for you to have a healthy and happy relationship that is buil on respect, it is important that they also know where they stand and when enough is enough – over time, if you are consistent witl these parenting messages, you will need to use them less but at first you do need to set the ground rules about behaviour at time: when they are with you in order for you to maximize the happy and fun times you have together in the longer term.

I feel judged and guilty because I am a full-time working mother.

And who is your biggest critic I wonder? I suspect for many parents who work, our biggest critic is ourselves, and, of course, as we have discussed so many times in the book, our perception of ourselves feeds straight into how we are in terms of our beliefs that underpin our thoughts, our feelings and ultimately our behaviour. So, if you feel guilty, this will impact on you in such a way that you will finding parenting more challenging and

raining and less of a pleasure. Furthermore, if you feel judged by
thers, you may want to question their motivation for this, which
 probably linked back to their own issues. Assess your situation –
 there are real adjustments you can make in order to maximize
our time with your child, do so, including making sure that when
ou are with them, you really are with them in mind, body and
pirit. Fundamentally, however, your child will be affected most
dversely by the way your feelings of guilt translate into your
nteractions with them, and that is what you must address.

o children with a stay-at-home parent develop etter emotionally and psychologically than those f working parents?

he quality of the relationship with the care-giver is key and
here are children who have stay-at-home parents who are
nhappy and children who have working parents who feel
appy and fulfilled, and vice versa. How we feel about ourselves
s people will impact on our abilities as parents and the nature
f our relationship with our children. The challenge for working
arents is to secure really good and loving childcare for when
ey are not with their children, and to ensure a home life
hereby the children feel valued, loved and respected and enjoy
gnificant and positive time with their parents. There are, of
ourse, children whose parents work and they see very little
f them and also children whose parents don't, but they are
onked in front of the TV all day – it's the quality of
nteraction that counts.

I have just been diagnosed with a terminal illness.
How do I prepare my children for my death?

Preparing children for death is a complex task that requires
all the instincts a parent can call on, plus a great deal of patience
and tolerance given that there might be some acting-up
behaviour. This is an extremely difficult task, particularly given
that you are also having to deal alone – and with your partner,
family and friends – with the enormity of what is to come. With
young children most families elect not to make the impending
death explicit but just to help the children understand that the
parent is ill. The reason for this is that very young children have
no real concept or understanding of the notion of death and
so will be confused and distressed about concepts that cannot
be explained to them adequately. Furthermore, for most families
it is important that all the time left together is spent in a way that
marks each moment with life rather than as one closer to death.
You may find comfort in writing letters to your children that they
can be given at key anniversaries or birthdays – these letters mean
that you still hold a role as their parent, communicating your
wishes, thoughts, advice and love for them even though you are
not there. I do think it is important to be honest with children
but I also believe that all honesty must be tempered by a real
understanding of whether the bald facts and knowledge will
help them or hinder them, and whether they are emotionally
and psychologically able to take on board the information they
are being given. Certainly, there are also charities that provide
support for families such as yours and also excellent and sensitive
children's books to help them understand when the time is right.

My mother is very critical of the way I bring up my children.

Our own experiences in childhood as well as our relationships with our parents can impact hugely on our perception of ourselves as parents and our ability to feel confident in our parenting. And just as we can find that these issues can come to the fore as we have children and grapple with the emotional aspects of being a parent, this can also be the case for our parents. Some grandparents can feel displaced by their grandchildren or even envious of the role they have in their child's (the parent's) life. For others there has been no adequate separation in their hearts and minds and they still view their child (the parent) as a child with all the issues that were always there. Others actually have some really great advice to give but this might not be received well either, because it is given in too critical or insensitive a manner or because we become too proud to hear it (which is a shame because it could hold a huge amount of helpful wisdom). Whatever the issue it is important to really think about what you are experiencing from your mother and whether that is truly coming from her or more from your own perception, based on your own issues with her. Whatever the reason, try and think it through in a manner that allows you to take a step back from the emotion and think about how you can discuss it with her without feelings being hurt or old arguments resurfacing. If this isn't possible, then it is important that you make your own boundaries round the relationship in a way that maximizes good and happy times for your child with their grandparent and enables you to cope with the comments.

I have recently left my aggressive and violent partner.
I have two young children from the relationship and I am
worried about their sometimes aggressive behaviour.

The term domestic violence includes physical, sexual,
psychological abuse as well as assault. Such violence is widespread
and occurs among all socio-economic groups. Children who have
experienced domestic violence feel helpless and traumatized, often
actively or passively trying to protect their mother (usually the
victim) and often getting caught in the 'crossfire'. They may feel
huge guilt that they were somehow responsible for the violence
and also can feel massively conflicting emotions towards their
victimized parent: those of blame and anger for the problem, for
not stopping it, alongside protectiveness and fear for their safety.

Most children will show greater anxiety, sometimes via physical
symptoms and psychosomatic illnesses, often saying they have
headaches or stomach aches. They can show clinical symptoms
of post-traumatic stress disorder and may have flashbacks and
nightmares. Some children can become withdrawn and regress
in their behaviour. Others may go the other way and become
aggressive themselves. For both these reactions understand that
they are underpinned by anxiety, and a very anxious child will
either show a fight (e.g., aggression, tantrums, rebelliousness,
treating a pet cruelly) or flight response (e.g., reduced social
contact, becoming non-verbal, regressed behaviour such as
poor sleep, bed wetting), often a combination of the two.

I have worked with families where siblings may 'act out'
what they have seen with violent play – one child often being
the perpetrator, the other the victim. Behaviourally, it is common
to see destructiveness and lashing out, outburst behaviour where
children are (a) anxious and (b) have problems with impulse
control, given the role modelling of aggression by their violent
parent. Finally, it is very common that when children are out of th

abusive home situation their behaviour can become more out of control – their way of expressing their distress and confusion in an environment without fear of punishment.

Children need a combination of time and space to express and process what they have experienced, plus clear loving and assertive non-violent boundaries around behaviour. When little children are anxious or angry it can be helpful to encourage them to find a way to verbalize what they are feeling via colours. With older children I have used red cards which they will hold up to their parent as a way of communicating that they feel their rage is overwhelming them; with little ones a traffic light system where they can point to the traffic light that shows how bad they are: green – I feel OK; orange – things are starting to feel horrid; red – I am getting very cross and want to hit someone. This simple mechanism enables them to feel some mastery over their feelings and can often diffuse a situation by giving you, the parent, time and space to take them to a quiet space and cuddle them while they talk, often cry, about whatever it is that has made them anxious or frustrated. Even when they are telling you that they hate you, tell them that you love them and understand that you are a safe person for them to vent their distress onto. They then should get lots of praise for talking about their feelings and not showing them physically.

Also encourage them to draw or paint or play out what they are feeling: reflect back to them what you see and ask your child to help you understand. Praise, patience and cuddles are very important, as are clear consquences when the behaviour gets out of control so that they learn what behaviour is unacceptable and harmful or disruptive to others.

A final note

We could fill pages and pages with further questions but I think by now we have exhausted a good range of queries that reflect the variety of ways we as parents can think about our children, their behaviour and our responses, and ultimately get to a point of understanding that is without anxiety, guilt, blame and argument.

I have really enjoyed writing this book as it has felt more like a communication from me to you on a personal level rather than some academic tome or slick and glossy technique-driven childcare manual (I've written both of those as well!). I really hope that you turn the final pages feeling inspired by the possibilities that lie ahead of you as a parent – possibilities that will also include challenges at developmental moments (yours and your child's) when life feels tough, frustrating and bewildering.

Most importantly, I hope that I have succeeded in taking the child-expert status away from people like me and have given it back to you in relation to your child. This expertise can only come from your intuitive connection to your child and the central and fundamental place you have in their life and they in yours.

In fact, it might be that as you reflect on the real difficulties that you've had, the stress you've felt and all the other really difficult emotions that you may have experienced with and about your child, you can now see – by asking you to look at yourself and to challenge aspects of yourself that could be so much more positive and fulfilled – how they bring so much to you. Children's behaviour can be very annoying and frustrating at times, but so can ours as adults – the difference is, however, that we have the benefit of experience and have had the chance to develop emotional self-management and social skills – they clearly haven't

So the next time your little one begins to turn up the temperature of everyone around them, take a step back, take a deep breath and, if you can, see these moments as times when you are being told in a very primitive and honest way that things don't feel right. Assess what you think is going on – maybe it's omething very simple that needs an assertive response so your child knows where they stand, or something more complicated hat requires the adults to look at themselves honestly and to ddress some bigger issues.

Whatever you conclude, YOU conclude and you manage ccordingly with love, respect and clarity because you parent our child YOUR WAY.

RESOURCES

Pregnancy

Antenatal Results and Choices (ARC)
Provides support and information to
parents during the antenatal testing process.
Tel: 0207 631 0285

BirthChoiceUK
Offers information for women on where
to have their baby.
www.birthchoiceuk.com

Citizens Advice Bureaux (CAB)
Advice on issues including pregnancy.
www.citizensadvice.org.uk

**fpa (formerly Family Planning
Association)**
Provides confidential advice on sexual
health, contraception, emergency
contraception and pregnancy options.
Tel: 0845 310 1334

Maternity Alliance
Campaigning, research, training and
information on maternity services
and rights.
Tel: 0207 490 7638

National Childbirth Trust
Information and advice on pregnancy,
breastfeeding and looking after babies.
Tel: 0870 444 8708

Tommy's
Advice on improving the chance
of a healthy pregnancy.
Tel: 0870 777 3060

Parenting

Association of Breastfeeding Mothers
Voluntary organization run by mothers.
There is a twenty-four-hour helpline to
a qualified breastfeeding counsellor.
Tel: 0870 401 7711

Breastfeeding Network
Information and articles about
breastfeeding.
Tel: 0870 900 8787

Dad's UK
Helpline for single fathers.
Tel: 0709 239 1489

Family and Parenting Institute
Information and advice from leading
experts.
Tel: 0207 424 3460

Families Online
Provides features and articles for families
of young children.
www.familiesonline.co.uk

Family Nurturing Network (FNN)
Group programmes for families of
children aged two to twelve.
Tel: 01865 791 711

Fathers Direct
Advice for fathers on parenting.
www.fathersdirect.com

Gingerbread
Organization for single-parent families.
Tel: 0800 018 4318

Grandparents' Association
Provides an advice line for queries relating
to grandparenting.
Tel: 0845 434 9585

HomeDad
Offers information and advice and
puts stay-at-home dads in contact with
each other.
Tel: 0775 254 9085

La Leche League
Helpline for breastfeeding mothers.
Tel: 0845 120 2918

Meet-a-Mum Association (MAMA)
Provides friendship and support
to mothers.
Tel: 0208 768 0123

**National Council for One
Parent Families**
Works to promote the welfare and
independence of single parents.
Tel: 0207 428 5400
Helpline: 0800 018 5026

One Parent Families Scotland
Information, resources and links
for and about single-parent issues.
Tel: 0131 5 563 899

Practical Parenting Advice
Information on family relationships and
child behaviour. Online parenting course.
www.practicalparent.org.uk

Raising Kids
Advice and information regarding
raising kids.
www.raisingkids.co.uk

**Twins and Multiple Births Association
(TAMBA)**
Information and support networks
for multiple-birth families.
Tel: 0800 138 0509
www.tamba.org.uk

Childcare

4Children
National organization for
out-of-school care.
Tel: 0207 512 2100

Childcare Link
Government resource, giving
information on national and local
childcare and early education.
Tel: 0800 096 0296

Daycare Trust
The national childcare campaign.
Provides information to parents,
employers and providers.
Tel: 0207 840 3350

**National Childminding Association
of England and Wales**
Advice on how to find a registered
childminder in your area.
Tel: 0800 169 4486

**National Council of Voluntary Child
Care Organizations (NCVCCO)**
The umbrella organization for voluntary
childcare organizations in England.
Tel: 0207 833 3319

Pre-School Learning Alliance
National educational charity and umbrella
body linking 17,000 community-based
pre-schools.
Tel: 0207 697 2500

SureStart
Government initiative to help families
prepare children for school.
Tel: 0870 000 2288

Talking Point
Information on speech and language
development.
Tel: 0207 674 2799

Working Families
Legal helpline that helps parents to
balance work and home life. Provides
information on parental leave and
childcare.
www.workingfamilies.org.uk

Healthcare

Action for Sick Children
The UK's leading children's
healthcare charity.
Tel: 0208 542 4848

**Enuresis Resource and
Information Centre**
Provides advice for parents
of incontinent children.
Tel: 0845 370 8008
www.eric.org.uk

**Foundation for the Study
of Infant Deaths**
Works to prevent cot death and promote
baby health to parents and professionals.
Tel: 0870 787 0554

Institute of Child Health
Research into the study and treatment
of childhood disease.
www.ich.ucl.ac.uk

NHS Direct
Free telephone and advice service
providing access to health information.
Tel: 0845 4647

Safety

Bullying Online
Information and advice for parents
and their children.
Email: help@bullying.co.uk
www.bullying.co.uk

Child Accident Prevention Trust
National charity committed to reducing
the number of children killed, disabled
and injured as a result of accidents.
Tel: 0207 608 3828

Kidscape
Charity that aims to prevent bullying
and child abuse.
Tel: 0845 120 5204

NSPCC
Charity devoted to child protection.
Tel: 0808 800 5000

www.britkid.org
Focuses on the issues of race and racism
and is aimed at schools.

Support and counselling

Association for Post Natal Illness
Offers information and support for
post-natally depressed mothers.
Tel: 0207 386 0868

Association of Child Psychotherapists
Provides details of accredited child
psychotherapists.
Tel: 0208 458 1690

Bliss
Premature baby charity offering a parental
support and advice network.
Tel: 0500 618140

**British Association for Counselling
and Psychotherapy**
Provides details of local counsellors
and psychotherapists.
Tel: 0870 443 5252

British Psychological Society
Holds national register of chartered
psychologists.
Tel: 01162 549 568

The Child Bereavement Trust
Offers support to bereaved parents
and children.
Tel: 0845 357 1000

Childline
Free twenty-four-hour helpline for
children and young adults.
Tel: 0800 1111

The Compassionate Friends
Organization set up by and for
bereaved parents.
Tel: 0845 123 2304

Cruse Bereavement Care
Help for bereaved people of any
age through counselling, advice
and mutual support.
Tel: 0870 167 1677

Cry-sis
Helpline for parents with excessively
crying, sleepless and demanding children.
Tel: 020 7404 5011

Home-Start
Support from parent volunteers
for parents of children under five.
Tel: 0800 068 6368

It's Not Your Fault
Website from NCH, the children's
charity, offering information and
support to children whose parents
are divorcing or separating.
www.itsnotyourfault.org

The Miscarriage Association
Support for those who have suffered
the loss of a baby during pregnancy.
Tel: 01924 200 799

**National Society for Children
and Family Contact**
Free support and advice for families
when a relationship breaks down.
Tel: 0870 766 8596

Parentline Plus
Free twenty-four-hour helpline for
parents, step-parents and carers.
Tel: 0808 800 2222

Relate
Provides couple counselling.
Tel: 01788 573 241
Helpline: 0845 130 4010
Counselling service: 0870 601 2121

Samaritans
Provides twenty-four-hour confidential
emotional support for those experiencing
feelings of distress or despair.
Tel: 0845 790 9090 (UK)
Tel: 1850 609090 (RoI)

**Stillbirth and Neonatal Death
Society (SANDS)**
Provides support for parents whose
baby died at or soon after birth.
Tel: 0207 436 5881

Supportline
Confidential telephone helpline offering
emotional support on any issue to children,
young adults and adults.
Tel: 0208 554 9004

Traumatic Stress Clinic
Offers a specialist approach to the
psychological assessment and treatment
of children and their families following
a trauma.
Tel: 020 7530 3666

**United Kingdom Council for
Psychotherapy (UKCP)**
National register of psychotherapists.
Tel: 0870 167 2131

Special needs

Asperger's Syndrome Foundation
Email: info@aspergerfoundation.org.uk
www.aspergerfoundation.org.uk

Contact a Family
Offers advice and support to parents of
children with special needs and disabilities.
Tel: 0808 808 3555

Council for Disabled Children
Information for parents regarding services
and support for disabilities and special
educational needs.
Tel: 0207 843 1900

Disabled Living Foundation
Help and advice on equipment for
older and disabled people.
Tel: 0207 289 6111

Disabled Parents Network
Organization for disabled people
who are parents or who are planning
to become parents.
Tel: 0870 241 0450

Down's Syndrome Association
Provides information, counselling and
support for people with Down's syndrome,
their families and carers.
Tel: 0845 230 0372

Gifted Children's Information Centre
Assessment of gifted, dyslexic, left-handed
children or adults, or those with Asperger's
syndrome or ADHD. Offers counselling
and advice for parents.
Tel: 0121 705 4547

Hyperactive Children's Support Group
Charity offering help and support to
hyperactive children and their families.
Tel: 01903 725 182

MENCAP National Centre
Charity that campaigns for equal
rights for children and adults with
a learning disability.
Tel: 0207 454 0454

**National Association for
Gifted Children**
Trains teachers, encourages parents
and educates administrators and
policymakers on how to develop
and support gifted children.
Tel: 01908 673 677

**The National Attention
Deficit Disorder Information
and Support Service**
Tel: 0208 906 9068
Email: info@addiss.co.uk

The National Autistic Society
Tel: 0845 070 4004

Young Minds
Promotes mental health of children
and young adults.
Tel: 0800 018 2138

ABC DIARY
Day

Time	
Antecedent (What triggered the behaviour e.g. Where are you? Who are you with?)	
Behaviour (What is happening? What did your child do?)	
Consequence (How did you respond? What did you do?)	
Outcome	

Day

Time	
Antecedent (What triggered the behaviour e.g. Where are you? Who are you with?)	
Behaviour (What is happening? What did your child do?)	
Consequence (How did you respond? What did you do?)	
Outcome	

SLEEP DIARY
Day

Morning waking time	Times of naps (if appropriate)	Time to bed	How you got your child to sleep	Time to sleep	Time(s) woke in the night	How you got your child back to sleep	Time back to sleep

TOILETING DIARY

Day, date and time	Wet or soil?	Where did it happen?	What did your child do?	What did you do?	Outcome

FOOD DIARY
Day

Time			
Meal, snack or drink			
What you gave and how much			
What the child has eaten and where			
Length of meal			
What the child did			
What you did			

INDEX

object permanence 45–6
operant conditioning 33
speech development 206
   and dummies 196
   onset of language 44
   stammering 204
   see also **toddlers**
transitional object 194–5
discipline
   holding your child
     and crying 199–200
   in a tantrum 77
   naughty stair 77
   smacking 72, 77
   Time Out 72–5, 77, 78
   see also **sticker charts**;

eating 109–122
   balanced diet 115, 121
   behaviour problems 86–7,
     110, 202–3
   calorie levels 115
   drinks 102, 113, 133
   food phobias 110, 115, 119,
     201–2
   fussiness 110, 118, 201
   mealtime routine 113, 115
   messy eating 119, 180
   obesity 109, 122
   parental attitude 112–13,
     114, 116–21
   physical problems 114
   presentations before food
     accepted 118, 202
   refusal 47, 50, 110
   self-feeding 115, 117, 119
   and sleep 94
   snack times 113, 115
   sticker charts 120
   and tantrums 86–7
   weaning 115
emotions
   anxiety 50–55
   child's awareness of
     parents' emotional
     issues 159–60
   and domestic violence
     222–3
   frustration 43–4, 65, 207–8
   parents' emotional issues

     145–50
   projection 159–60
   shyness 192–3
   see also **anxiety**;
     projection

family
   agreeing about what
     should be changed 67
   birth order 212
   blended families 215–16
   child behaviour and family
     problems 151–3
   child labelled as a problem
     38
   child's perception of his
     role 38–9
   extended 155–6
   grandparents 221
   middle-child syndrome
     212
   mixed projections – mixed
     messages 170–71
   nuclear 155
   one parent has a new
     partner 216–18
   powerful child 25, 155,
     156, 157
   sharing process of
     behavioural change 40
   siblings
     death of an older sibling
       162
     hitting 62–3
     and sleep behaviour 104
     toddler and a new sibling
       47, 48, 65, 212–13
     at war with each other
       214–15
   single parents
   structure 154–6
   trans-generational patterns
     157, 161
   fears *see* **anxiety**
   food *see* **eating**

games *see* **play**
grandparents *see* **family**

health
   ADD (Attention Deficit
     Disorder) 204–5
   ADHD (Attention Deficit
     Hyperactivity
     Disorder) 204–5
   autism 208
   colic 200
   cranial osteopathy 200
   diet, importance of 109,
     201–2
   exercise, and tantrums 86,
     87
   GAD (Generalised Anxiety
     Disorder) 190
   obesity 109, 122
   physical disabilities 207–8
   PND/ PNI (post-natal
     depression/illness) 79,
     163–4
   post-traumatic stress
     disorder 222
   stress
     child's 50
     parental 48, 49, 50, 51,
       53, 54, 161
   see also **emotions**; **anxiety**;
     psychology

learning *see* **development**
life events
   abuse 165–7
   birth of a new sibling 212–3
   death
     of an older sibling 162
     preparing child for death
       of a parent 220
   divorcing or separating
     parents 209
   domestic violence 222–3
   parent
     meeting/introducing a
       new partner 216–17

Acknowledgements

This book has been written with the enormous support and encouragement of so many at Penguin and Michael Joseph – in particular my editor and chocolate-biscuit dealer Kate Adams, the very patient Sarah Rollason and the boss lady Louise Moore. Also thanks to Katy Szita, Smith & Gilmour, Jacq Burns, Kipper Williams for his amazing cartoons and Samantha Mackintosh for her brilliant copy-editing.

I met many parents who gave their time to discuss what they thought a book like this needed – I hope I have realized their wishes and thank them hugely for their invaluable and honest insights.

I am privileged to have met and worked with hundreds of children, young people and their families during my clinical career. My experiences with them all have, I hope, enabled me to think beyond a clinical training and place theory amongst real human experience. Within my career I have worked with many brilliant colleagues and am especially indebted to Dr Wendy Casey, who trained and mentored me during my early career, whose comments on the first draft of this book were as always so detailed and helpful.

Finally huge thanks to my best friend and business partner Sam 'Doris' Richards and most especially to my amazing husband Bruce and our gorgeous children Lily and Jack who think that it is hilarious that I have written this book.